The Road - A Start

The asphalt and crushed chinese bones, I lay my ear to the rails, my finger wet to the air, to feel that ramble under the hood, the miles under rubber and flood for a lass of an engine with one more intake of thoroughfare, one more jubilant penniless hurrah, starving and burdened by nothing more than the passing of signs, the warmth of new vessels, and the hopes for a fruitful year. Seasonally we've transpired a move up and down these coasts, our fruits bursting or rotten, trailing the old maps laid out and ruined on the quivering lacerated cement of our American dreams.

Every year the autumn tree turns over its youth to the fire of its predecessors, and strangles within itself the chlorophyll of self desire, to lease the earth a compost of its heat, to be naked and steadfast amongst the chilling winds of winter, to prove it remains within its rings alive for the spring.

The untiring tyranny of the travelled path beaten harsh with the wayward posts of a season of ice or fire, the maligned winds of change that fossils an extinct species into the granular display of reach, this is the infinite matter that constitutes our search, our will to move forward. Aging cartographers with our simple beat of blood and oil, to map and remap again.

It leaves the reputable oaks key to freely govern their anchored abodes with words of wisdom or sighs mooring themselves to this knowledge, that the journey is from inside, and the winds are always whispering with their thirsty tinge of seas salt and spit. And comfortable they pine away at sapling lust, waiting it out in the fields that they have conquered, minding their hands in time to populate a lasting germination, and in due time to culminate their will in flowers.

The dilemma thus can be found in growth, for everyone in manner of nature seizes on the soil such to procure their kin, to manifest ones strength in patience, all along indifferent to the rising sparks aglow hesitant but creeping on the horizon, for consumption of fuel leaves these beauteous stalwarts as a sitting ambition, an easy thrill of rapid advance to augment ones own peaceful consignment to the tender of another souls furnace moving down a new found road.

This populous of movement is driven by resources, to replenish ones own used up sense of identity, to lavish about motionless when these inputs tend to falter is to gain within oneself the nerve of forever, for forever never comes.

For when that light of fire dwindles, nothing but the darkness can be seen, and the light of the stars appears to rejoin us to the universe which never lost sight of this constant flowing, the ebb and flow of supernova, the fission and fusion of our own known forever cycles.

I step outside into the frigid twinkle of this, huddle my shaking bones around another cigarette, bringing this fire closer to my face, and I look to the road one more time, to find for myself what we set out for in the first place, to replenish and to abandon, to seek, for we have yet to ascertain why.

One goes on in these cycles of forever.

Thus
Virginia
Passes

poems by

James Browning Kepple

pretend genius [press]

London, New York, San Francisco, Seattle, Washington D.C.

Published simultaneously in the United States and Great Britain in 2012
by Pretend Genius Press
London, New York, San Francisco, Seattle, Washington D.C.

ISBN 978-0-9852133-2-9

For Levi, Betty & Virginia

Introduction

Here is a book of American Verse. Uncut, raw. Let this be an invitation and a warning. If you've come expecting that carefully compressed poetics where beauty is synonymous with that which must be severed from all excess: the ugly, the repetitive, the political, the internet, the disorienting and decadent noise of our so-called information age, then you shall be duly disappointed.

There is nothing refined about *Thus Virginia Passes*, nothing contained or moderated. Here are too many poems, crammed together, at times it will seem, unbearable. Because it is. A distinctly American poetics in the tradition of the individual lodged in the system, armed with a language that is always disappearing, that must be reinvented, reborn, wrestling itself for air, breathing through its smallest components with a restless, pulsating defiance.

Consider Thoreau's neck-beard and Crane's fatal fondling. None of the 90 poems in this collection knows a "blank page" nor accepts as a response "contemplation". The search for beauty is never against but always amidst, one-eye to the road, that great beyond, and the word-noise, always moving, bustling at the heart of human intersections.

Whether writing from a tent in West Virginia, as in *Book I: Thus Virginia Passes*, or from a bar-stool in Harlem, *Book II: Harlem Blues*, or even from that fevered asylum in the sky that makes up *Book III: Herald*, the James Browning Kepple experiment remains the same, which is to say, human, which is to say, faulty, which is to say, corruptible but also capable of great love, humor, madness, landscape, and tragedy.

-Kim Göransson. Virginia, 2012

Contents

Book I: Thus Virginia Passes

Book II: Harlem Blues

Book III: Herald

Book I: Thus Virginia Passes

virginia I hardly knew you
in the red hair of your mountains
never heard your sweet coos
from the heights of your williamsburg

I often in secret corridors of highway
would incant you in steed for no steam,
you were neutral, violent
and I hardly wrestled you

Paraplegic Marine

I've left out the dog in the rain,
its famished wet fur
is scattered on the lawn,
its freezing to death,
I can see it gnarl from its chained position
those squawky chipmunks and squirrels

he is dying slowly under the elements,
he has lost his canine vocabulary
and cannot enchant the smell of groin
to lead a poodle or a chihuahua to unleash,
picktooth this machination hold him to death
squandered rabies roars and pelted doneout

for all dogs must go down the red fern valley,
to choose for themselves which master is mortality,
the buckeyed cherry bark of grotesque rotgut,
the carved out lament in pine shouldering shelves,
we place on our hindquarters to push ass to feeble
paraplegic marine come home

all of you merrily enjoying this, your information,
your warmth of parasol in balcony seats,
for this unplead saturate victim in opera desperatior
loads up your cameraphone before you call police,
animal control, the supreme justices of our capital
to lay lead into the dying dogs

foregone pup dog child of tricks, theres no more comfort in
        bitches,
we've leased our greatest endowed plans in sweaty comfort,
hid our blood swollen conquests in the seeds of youth,
for those outposts have yet closed shelter, tender shelter
after killing many a man, they wish us to grow up and be one,
slaughtered glue and rust covered shotgun burst

can we rescind
forget about all these pasts and slowly go into the night,
foragers of the unkind protest of the rapid industrial male,

a fractured human
or am I the only observer of our mammals resistance
being laid asunder in a position of power to cease,
as a dissenter
I saw a girl in truck she had a bumper sticker,
this glued on thought our new literature,
if you do not love America give it back,
and I wish so much to give her my Oklahoma,
tracing her bellybutton lint a teared trail

distract these elements, do not oxidize your own ore,
raise up and yolk ravished strungup compatriots,
give a common human purpose to this madness,
we are all wounded unthought banished scavengers,
held by chain under the command of ugly fat denizens
that we worship

the dog spirit roaming, the nomadic grit of buffalo hunted,
the peacemaking in silenced breath,
do ordain this a striking moment of courage
where we will impart the colonized bow,
engage catgut sinew to unleash missile
into the belly of the freedom destroying man

stand up you paraplegic marine, unleash

Wake

Surrender to the rainy
Allegheny
your shuddering frozen
bones,
lesson this cold kept
mountainous tent retreat,
the fresh air of the bubbling
brook in tone our ode,
a life cut from sapling
broken by hand
to be tossed on fire,
do we thus warm our souls

Forgive the egotism of
your churning knucklehead
mush of a brain
for a needed old man
to be whistling pines in comfort,
deems hard work thus sown now
in the post formative
ascent of age
For you are but wet wood,
no charcoal starter,
a long laborious hard study
do we gain from the natives,
the Neanderthals to bring forth
to the sky our smoke signals humble
non deluded, not self interest
these lashings of discontent,
the small simple smell of her hair
for you and no other
is all in heat we should bring
and not ask for the meteor of destruction
taking penance of one self
for the sins of others,

the evil eye
the look
the keeping up with misses
and mr. jones
                    ATONE!

breathe in one's own simple steam
born forth from a beating muscle
this mass do we thus condense
and sort out the ventricle of being
within our own humanimality,
to let the others perish precipitous
under their own wet of thought,

altruism is not for suckers
but a close moment of battle
so picked to fight in lieu
of one taking on the world

for hidden in this discourse
proves our simple good intent,
to make good on ones efforts,
or youre just a stinking phoney
left out in the cold woods
alone

after midafternoon gin

the moon will come out surely as it has on occasion early,
hang like the left out cheese pinned to string in bathroom,
why I ask do you have such a device, so, well prominent,
she responds coyly, so I don't feel bad about locking the kitten in,
I surveyed the sleeping cat on bed, she purred her spatial climb,
dreaming notable about one day capturing this pungent orbit,

when I fell asleep last night, the girl perused my torso with her nose,
I have a finely attuned sense of smell, and you my dear, smell of
            death,
and I don't like that fact, so I'm going to shower now and sleep,
some would offer alternatives, maybe an ocean side cruise in car,
maybe start on that new fantastic novel we've all been hearing
            about,
I long to derange the face of the man staring me in the mirror,
cut it up nicely as to be recognizable only to the new man inside

I don't wish to die just yet, for I do not wish to be a lousy subhuman
complaining about the moon on a string,
I only want love, I'm tired of couches in this fashion
the not quite good enough louse that snores too long or too loud,
for all of us feel deserving of another in our quest
whether that be for food or milk, all this talk of moons
and unrequited mercy fucks, nasal clinical opinions and feline
ambivalence

for us too wish to rile the moon with our talons
and to sharpen our leap, to cleanse our nail to reach and tear out a
            figment
in the sky,
calls for the more subversive,
the more of the more of the more that we are capable of
and lonely I bathe, for if not my own smell,
then what else can I take?

old rusty parts

tools, pieces, wheels
oxidizing, ruining, covered in grease
I hand over a wrench
he plies it through the ventricle,

you know you boys should play some of that ol segregation
music,
I shrug my shoulders
hes probably right,
turn over my engine, and it starts right back up

my eyes are like the creaking red wilt of metal
left out in the kansas sun, broken open fine iron,
no longer impenetrable, no longer shiny, dull, cracking useless
pull down my ruined coveralls to a scene alone, overweight

to sleep such horrible sweats and meaningless omens of time,
rusty old parts tossing the sheets,
do I toss back another meaningless aluminium to prepare
again
for one more doleful rest, I no longer wish to repeat

and the dreams, they tell me stories I ignore
that once useful sense of industry finds a ruined scarecrow,
a listless blow of the dandelion
where seeds land on gravel and grow

will the humble poet stand

up for the good fight?

for you do not wish
now to be devoid
of poetry

for you need now
that mystic energy
to help influence the
battle against technology
mechanized humans
and lay not the blame
on the state of things
for the poets in theory
will have alot of hardships
before they have had
enough, and its
the poets you need,
to survive our species

not our continued culture
not the same life
never again we'll
live no life so careless & pompous
with the soil, it has
decided to join in on the
fight itself, to know
what a rock is made
of pelted by us
predators

For in the dust annals of ode
you will find all the signs that
we all our travelling a road
unknown, & that freedom
not comfort is
what make a poet whole

Holy,
a flashing fountain
full of bullets
puddling the ground

Down the Foibe

was the last time I saw you
and it was there in trieste
that we felt this way, falling
to the sad swoon of the sea

thrown from the gulf
both of us in free communal
bound by tongue our caress
our love broken

Down the Foibe
in the darkness
chasms of our limbs
and our hands can connect

recapitulate, get up
torn from stars, strive
our love above
and throw ourselves back

paper table poem

I satiate at the bar,
linger in brine,
pickle my liver,
enjoy the sordid
matter of affairs
broadcasting over
the television, I hide
a secret, embrace
it under shirt,
giggle at the overheard
conversation and sink
within myself to the
deep pounding of
rachmaninov,
lonely, drink, silent
do I dare to speak

on this paper table,
I watch you

your hair is pulled back
the way that I would have
you comb your hair in my presence,
back, like the motherly tones of comfort
that holds your beauty up
through the work of the day

I long for the moment that we can coalesce
in the dark and let your hair down
over our family, cascade down your bodice
to hide your nefarious nipples,
dark as chocolate as silk in my mouth
I envy our children,
sucking on you for milk,
I long for you in this way

The beach, he returneth

tony the red swam through the murky shallow waves,
stood sideways, toes perked in sand
dancing with the ebb and flow of jellyfish

he was caught in the glisten of surf,
his white flesh reflecting the sun,
it shone off of his brightly painted red star

as all the women watched
they bustled about borsht, anal sex, the lot,
kept dribbling on with such cunt.

tony launched himself with the water
flipping over and landed on the beach feet to the sea,
laughed, curled himself out and up

these rituals had been practiced for years
and it had been that since he had seen brighton beach,
tony was fresh out of the joint with an ankle bracelet

it was a beacon
it grew hot with the sun
and burned his leg

he limped almost with a flourish,
toes nibbling away at this hallowed ground,
retreated to his long sleeve shirt and trousers

mentioned a passing dostradona to the senoritas giggling in bikini,
trudged back up the alleyway to his fathers apartment,
tipped his hat at the doorman and went on in

he had been worked out on the stair machine, now it was his world
          cup,
glided up the 20 flights to his somber oft used home,
knocked on the door

"Tony!" he was greeted, arms around each other,
shots of vodka were poured, and tony borrowed his fathers knife,
pulled out a bag of heroin and sliced it open

"Tony, its so good to have you back, we have missed you darling"
he knew they were telling the truth, snorted,
wiped his nose with the blade, "Nostrovia" and downed a shot

"So dearest," his mother cooed, "won't you stay for dinner"
Tony hadn't said but two words, stood up and went to his old room,
uncovered underneath the wooden floor his lucky syringe

tied his communist arm to the job
shot back
and slept on his childhood bed to dream

To die under a big sun

I always adored my son there on the lawn
his stance on riding mower always helve curvature
of spine upright in the morrow moments of heat,
there we smell the crass shorn,
there we drink and salt our lips
for the sweat to equal pint, as children we groan
hide our feet to the sweeping cuts of sweep
nah,
green is for the genius, I am but enjoying the cut in half
the sweet release of death that renews in dew
our catch of breath, happy
uncharted uncut, to the flow of green
that falls as if carpet between our toes

Farewell Roanoke

You star city of the south, you forgotten colony of
          Raleigh,
god has cursed you in your supple mountains,
in your secluded coasts of Carolina,
has left you barren with aged women, their skin
          dried out and stretched like
bison skulls hidden under the thin layer of railroads
          that straddled you,
indian pockmarks and fevered blankets,

I have worn your supplies, have imbibed in your
          ales and snow,
harboured my hooded deception through your
          townsquare market,
always sheathed and hidden in dagger I have
          wandered your dismantled
buildings with a keen eye as to my departure, and
          to leave you there,
desolate, cold, alone

a good nature in laugh always led you to ask what
          had brought me there,
for I have recorded diligently in my soft tissue of
          brain,
channelled your lessons through a pipe organ,
wrote of the bounties outstretched all around you
          but for you,
dear Roanoke, will always be abandoned,
a colony of indifference, your people disposed

as outpost you have coddled dire frequencies of sos,
          muted peddlings of morse,

trying to usurp the saddle of belief from even the
        strongest,
we scrawl on your wooden cornerstone our last
        breathings
unfinished, unrelinquished of stress,
you have bludgeoned our heads with distaste and
        disgust
and yet you wonder why all the children turn out so
        misshapen,
your felines and hoarded holes of warmth with filth

oh roanoke! your misfortunes run deep!

and so we continue onward from your shell,
the hollowed out hope you have forsaken
and run forward and outward through the fields of
        regrowth
and leave you here, the beaten prostitute of youth,
to wallow in her broken vessel,
to cry herself to sleep under the mountains of
        sorrow,
a shivering recluse cut up and dire

for somewhere there must be a god of want
in your shuddering self I hope you pray to discover,
farewell dear Roanoke

train poem #43

I only
write on the
trains,
& I hate
the trains
but its all I have

I'm still anonymous
here, maybe
you look like
the blues brother,
I am all the
blues brothers,
in pen they at
least acknowledge
in a good way,
that its the new
ipod game
writing, so I'm
sneaking up

& thats just plain
great to me
& I'm fucking
great at it

aha!
I've found
a cheap
plastic bic
I trust
and my
chest pocket
is beating
the pdas,
Beating them!

eyes like
beacon jaguar,

the fur of her
jacket raises
up & the mouth
has things
unsaid to me,
but I can
tell shes
not happy,
fluttering
there in boots
I think
she is on to
me, I can
smell it in
her scent,
a troubled
troubadour
lashed about
in train seat,
she can walk
like fallen
plastic on my
feet

The outside of my

summer tent is
covered in snow,
I'm hobbling over a
propane tank in
5 layers of clothings,

I wonder somehow it must
have been, alas we will
never know, but experience
again

the lost art of seduction

I lost you there at the mini cooper and laundromat
I asked did you want to sit on the machine?
you say nah I'm just trying to get home
take care of my girl

shes a little old for that,
and this pbr is getting kinda of warm,
why dont you kiss me again,
I lost the art of seduction she says

and now were sexting,
and I instruct her to vibrate her self
w/each sms, like my side burns
on her thigh I text

I tell her I'm hungry
ask, or is that to caveman

I stole a piss in the graveyard

the former northern most point of Norfolk
I hid behind a giant tree
the cold marble heroes laid down in front of
the freemason built catholic church

to lead way down the elizabeth river
past the hippies standing in line
to the one dollar coors light life of waiting
for prostitutes to finish off their fat clients
of the republic, shitting on her back

this existence existential one compadre concedes
justifies the most rash of passion as to what one needs
to grab the fallen pecans from the landscaped headbones
crack a meaty morsel truth for own belly lint

nor covered in pamphlet or public service announcement
all traded for 1000 pounds of tobacco and casque
I have cornered the market on the hallowed land
first we thrust forth an ideology aggrandesized
non taxed wealth sailing port to port in search of
a supple injun hide to scalp and add to health
another soul raped, genealogy left for disease
the blanket of comfort they have constructed
to wander and wonder and wander and wonder

and this I dig from the spade of luck
who there with me in urn but ashes and books
to burn to signal a romance over seas
and incense a tribal god worship

that will bring down the plan of planes
as double bird shot to engine
we bring tea, marble masterpieces this steam
I stole a piss in the graveyard

Deer hit by truck survives

I've got a bonfire for ink
scribble here midnight
down by the river,
its cause I've been selling
wood all night, 90 mph
through mountain oneway
curves to speak to
travellers of fish,
egg em' on wood
a passenger, the
serial cold killer
with nothing but
swiss army knife
to the sidearms
of man

the bonfire, no matter
how much oak or
pine, or cherry, I throw
samson, gets
bigger, god damn
night time scribble
light, & you should
see such handwriting
tetris the last of
word, & boy howdy
did we carry it,
speaking osama bin
nigger burning up the
fuel prices, go clown
up to the main left fork

the main west fork
down by the bridge
now you follow
the small east
river to the west
fork & then up the
way is the main

left fork, deep
holes with rocks, that
you shimmy lime on top
then jig your way to trout
well what kinda
wood do you have,
pine, sawmill, cherry
& red oak,
well boy how much you
want for a couple
handfuls,
we load up the flammable
for old men to strap
on back & make
knife handles
round the curve
up the bend we
non seatbelt
will never
fall off mountain

for no one
falls off a
mountain

It just gets bigger

I have the largest
fire I've seen,
we run over a deer
a lucky one
laid on its belly
under the truck
for the bar was
closed no tender
loin skinnin'
but beer
and weed I sit
on a rock and watch
4 pallets waft stuck
top to top on the

last night of derby
do I 14 days latter
finally mingle with
the locals
for this is
a fire for 10
For Fire Forms
rock
& 10 of us
our fondling
round
formed
let it burn
deerless
hot as hell
you can put
the trout on the
cheery
there is no more
wood to throw

but wood!

carly

I met a carl sandburg girl
across the river from the factory,
I had but 5 pennies in my pants
and I skipped one on over
and she laughed at my aim,
I laughed at her age,
I saw her dip into her loins for a quarter,
she tossed me a tip,
I clasped the coinage

to buy pint

hilary

your gypsy fiddle breaks the night
howls through the eaves a torrid tear,
and bemoans to us in the acrid lure of summer
another morning, another cascade of the strings,
leaves us hungry tortured dreamless beings,
and we wander off into the wilderness blind,
searching for your succulent sound in ear

for we are greedy, we are desperate for a taste,
we wish to milk your pale skin of its ode,
take you down from your heavenly night throne
and worship you with our animal maul and teeth
for you have led us in siren an infected beast,
and for you to leash, we come ever hither
we shall wander blind through the darkest of times

and for you we take in the coal of virginia
for your children we shall hold a land aside,
and you keep playing so tender and meticulous
that we mustn't rest till we hear your sweet song,
and we shall sit at your threshold meek and latent,
satiated, gregarious and consumed by your melodies,
for this sweet hilary is where you must end your violin

and I can go in
go forward into you as rapid locusts in nile,
a heat born of such profound temperature
that we shatter the earth around us, our simple human flesh
        shudders,
and we thunder great cries of fire, together we scream our
        music,
and a muse and a queen share in pristine elegy
once upon a time, over and over, until we fall, exhausted

intertwined, sweaty, and you pick up your bow
to lead me astray
this way is how I need you
for my loins beg for your embrace
and all I have to do is listen in the night

for that bit of gypsy fiddle
and you know I'm yours on the way

occidental street love

you leave here early within my mind,
you leave in the morning,
you leave when the dolphins have perished,
you leave when we have nothing left

I leave sandalled and on hot pursuit,
I sit on the stoop, I wait for you to appear
but you never come when I am looking,
no nothing happens when I am keen,
you leave my memory this easy

and when the sun dopes up the horizon
we search for the starry eyed handle
to deal thus with such dilemmas,
and you are there in your crack whore
when I have nothing, not even 20 dollars

you say, you accost really, I am yours
I diddle with my phone,
I look for an excuse cause I'm not a millionaire
but I see those spunky tits inclined for tonight
and I pass her up wishing I wasnt so cheap

I suppose its a matter of money these encounters,
I try to budget and pass up on your sexual hounding
I regret almost always, these ships passing in night,
for I have worked so hard for such harbour
to bring my schooner within your dock, to weight
ocean in our petroleum dilute, in our hoary pursuit,
you gather and multiply, send out minions,
diversions for such a blight
and I can't seem a reason to stop and fight
outside you, your glory, your beauty in tit,
there in the sanctuary of the transcendent

we shall diversify our identity
and merge one in one on the coast of your sieve,
we shall coalesce such murderous waves on shore
our fondling of sheets, our toes violent in cotton

and nothing more then this do I want then to fall asleep,
and you say with your wicked toothpick
and you say with your knowing of my kind,
do not worry love, 20 to 25 and your mine
the chemistry of greats

shake it off

take the towel to the outback, shake it off,
let the potato strain through the twist of cloth,
wrangle out your polish demons,
for you are not dying in warsaw for stalin,
you stay strong here in the stone carved gargoyle
   vestibule,
you were put here to save yourselfs,
justify your struggles through terse travels and
   misbegotten love
and now to fall
in the fall of new york, stand in summer

its just a liquid, nah barnabee, its been a walk over,
and the hoverboard has been trashed,
they hold you neck high in canal, and ask where
your flippers have gone,
ask where now in this submerge you plan on prying
   yourself earth,
for truthfully my priest
for humbly my sun quest
I need this tear of canvass
this triumphant plod

shake it off, use the towel, we'll squeeze it out
rebottle, and burn the cloth
to launch big things,
to celebrate in life
after the wall of fire
a drink good man
and drink as much as you want
for you will have all the time to do so

really? nah you will probably be shot
down a lead tree laid stretch of road
but for now, do not die in a still
naked and useless,
you have mouths to feed
beaches to see
walls of water to cheat
and walk off

we've been left for dead

cursed few amongst us strewn
to the tides of the pacific highway,
to the now cleansed sandpipers tomb,
up the ancient eastern graven curves,
through the whistling pines and wheat
do we continue our small odes and elegy,
a swindled pile of oak smolder
through the surly cold of night,

a tempest restless yearning for warmth,
a closeness of ones body to creation,
do we wail out for holy champion
to guide us back to our humanity,
guide us back to the power in soul,

the nature of our lost phantasm,
branded sorcerers and storytellers
for this future is yet foretold

a factitious diary

left unsweltered there on the pier
do we stumble over tetanus cruciform,
shake off the droplets
and surmise it all with the sun sheltered
beneath your iris
hammered improperly

do not stumble
do not let your fear paralyze you here
in this vast snowy wool,
do not let the ink dry

to have been summoned by the gusts salty
down the bending curvature of riverbed
do we escape to the sea
do we escape to the sea

whiff up the sulfur, burn this overture
our washed away sense of indifference
to rejoin in the manner spoken,
a journal of our unheard mannerisms,
left revelations
and crawl within each other to die

blue

the eyes like glue
may just fall out this instant
for I'm tired of staring
surveying the curvature in elevation,
for i was not seeking a topical map
just a mere guide in dusty path
and what more do I receive then x,
here marks the spot we divulge,
hide deeply within our skirts of solitude
for not one man can well enough of this stain
that holds back the arch granite of hoover
and belittles the small villages below

oh so silly blue, the fish skip past fissure
find means for a dutchman to euthanasia
billy plum fingered out they figured and swam
hard and true to the freewheeling motion current,
oh how we so desire their fin of haste
to mourn ones lost of faith in freedom of self

travelling now in their submerged glorious birth
(thus we hide in the reefs)
come out now and again to catch and release
(run from the polebait)
for in probate concerns for wealth, food,
we digress a caulk sway of pinned up police

please monitor, please concern yourself
for I am but only one cock eyed walleye
found on stake in tucson for closure, escape,
a hearty beauteous spotted gill wallower
held up under dry sun, mounted on furnace
(and we wish for this new river in heat)
I'm so blue for you,
my dear escaped carp,
and not even this hollowed harmonica
can keep up in this solitary confinement
the tears you swim on
to borough out

Out of the Woods

There is a grander light as seen between the trees
As the mountain's bowl has encompassed me,
Coddled me with the sweet pleas of a robins sorrow
Gleeful cardinals and their early morning rise

To the efface of this, my own tent of a head
For too long the hoarded nuts have been given girth
So much so that I have leaked out acorns to the streets
Relinquished my wealth in sanguine sweat of dreams

For what has one gandered from this to come out of the woods
Alive and breathing new found future
All one has to do is work through the pain in the hand of scythe
To mow down the numerous thoughts that linger there

A gait of pure frivolity when the moment so calls for wine
A stride in the heat of the furnace, my toe numbing pine
Of ones escape into a coordinated flee, nigh' a full out gallop
Into the unknown territory you've been holding your breath for

And now young man with your Thoreau hat, your coals alive for the
        week,
Your tattered Chekhov in hand, may you find your sleep
I look to the Radio Telescopes, to the love of a woman
To come out of the woods, a radiotelegraphy of hope

For what has one gandered from this to come out of the woods
Alive and breathing new found future
All one has to do is work through the pain in the hand of scythe
To mow down the numerous thoughts that linger there

To come out of the woods, a radiotelegraphy of hope

jump passaic

the simple laugh & smile
churn the raceways of the
caged in passaic as I stare
down from the wooden planks
about the violent twisting
of the waters
might, I order
a hot dog, she
gives me another
jump another chance
to land without
danger in the
wet pools
of her flesh

I wish to indulge in the acts of gods,

they ask me what I want to do
I wish to indulge in the act of gods
to sheepish retreat, head down and 20 feet hook tied and swinging
our chains shall rally, our steeds shall secede
mexican pauses, latin stallions befouled

all of our water is sediment, all of our drops and soil dewed done
a canopy of hope remains in your fur, in your ballistic protrusions
the heat from ticks we rub and in candid blubber, silken sea trim
to condense
eat of canned produce
this suckered jab dulled tin

Thus Virginia Passes

Slowly, pulsing, beating
But surely
Under the whip of the ocean,
The trace of the seagull
The blood shorn rugged
Hardy and hungry for vinegar,

We are Holding out on cross
For flooded power expands,
Stretches sponge to mouth,
To hold ones diaphragm with bolt,
Steel a sanction of speech
And speak in pained disintegration,

For she's begging for remiss,
straddles us in duress
this atlantic pacific daunt,
a soft remembrance of kiss
left behind in breeze'd or'
mettlesome sand,

we offer up to the gods our morsels,
the intense bursts of our infrastructure
diluting our feverish moans,
the esters seeping our morning howls,

For We all must wait here for the pass
The cross pattern looming coast,
And down we drown their dilemmas,
This world of sanctions, resource

Threading field, lacing turf of ice,
Bounding on hardwood or asphalt
Sitting on stoops watching Detroit,
The faded phosphorous oh night

A gleam of barrels industrial
soiling our granules in sheen,

For We are being raped

Taking on the phone call in car,
Yes baby its gonna be just fine,
As long as you get pass dallas,
Onto Vermont, onto the east

Past the broken Kansas where Maryanne hoists
the last chicken coop to jalopy and closes up topeka,
our poor american ideals,
poor tears left desolate out in the chided chaff,
they are lying to you about our chinese hens,
leaving it for the dustbowl-
they are mowing down corn for concrete,

And all our fortunes sold in moments, minutes of stock,
Radio vascular tubes, burnt bulbs leather,
Our bulging back pockets dictate
A sitting,
An interlude in suburbs,
suburbans,
don't call me applebees
Call
me a just moment of repose,
for baby I just love the way you're harlem,
Your salty rebellious mouth
the acidic peach mold consume,
The spit on conventions
relaxed and walking such rope,
Call it quits, hurry in puffs,
Sequester big hearty groans
blackening lungs deep in our allegheny

Don't even talk
Not a word, for we have no tape,
No sticky,
Nothing to hold on to
As we venture further in this traipse ,
This lollygag oh dear, we're in America!

Snicker and walk proud down avenue,
Streets dirty with heat, sweat and hairgel,
A laundered flower of lily on chest
We divest in haberdasher, chink, lawnmower,
Cutting our protruding human in awe

an Owner malfunct, devoid of instruction,
the price to jettison our least,
to hide our fat,
Our faithful blind paramours of love,
Rhetoric, faith and population,
Above the naked astronaughts daughter,
The space in which to do so lies up,

Above her cosmic taste that we ingest,
Consume a fear pear past wall, barrier fence-
Peek over love, I can almost see you,
I can almost taste your tongue dance in mouth,
These are the stretches of giant jesus argentina
Impaled in massive statues of pain in Houston

We hold,

Virginia passes in will of defeat, lacking expansion,
The sojourn of oratory fed spoonful your eyes,
Your soft backwoods nature, tender untenderized,
Bawdy brilliant and collective spreading over this land
That we had

That we took

Our footsteps back into this hallowed niggerland
The parcelled acreage splintered
fleeced In seed, corn, and cotton,
I pull up my britches,
seek out pickles and booze,
Spend my verbs, Dialects of mumbled fast mouth hustle
we erect churches, achieve megaphone status outsice wards
waft it lone in bottle
washed up on to the lost shores of jamestown

decadent unrefined wanderlust,
a womb in birth, the beckoning call of such red ink distinction
between diapers,
love massages, sweet serenades and bills to pay, a crossbolt to
       one's headstone,
ones female embrace, you have already bound yourself to this
       stretch of terra terse
and you did not wish to grow up earth, you wished to stay,
plant seeds and everything kosher and ok

for I am no longer lingering for a hit,
a bit, a blast of granite for insight,
strange that it comes so late in life,
the need to defunct, pull away from such landing pad
soft and comfortable for predictive neuron condition,
spread legs out on couch & sleep well

Virginia, I hardly knew you
in the red hair of your mountains
never heard your sweet coos
from the heights of your williamsburg

I often in secret corridors of highway
would incant you in steed for no steam,
you were neutral, violent
and I hardly wrestled you

now I play with your lost street gangs,
I don't consult the book or memo my course,
I feel in this way I may be remiss,
but to rebirth, but to rebirth you-

transverse an acrid cacti call of the Sonora,
cash croon'd pipes rolling down tracks,
whistled out of lone smokestack onway bout silverton
for my grandmother booked passage
departed durango in a whiff of balefire

Virginia, our beautiful matriarch
full of soft smiles and austere love
you bore forth the pangs of earth for husband
whence victorious he returned from the great war

Virginia my grandmother is dying

she's up the potomac, a vessel in flame, a vase of ceremony
shenandoah she falls in mesa, my sisters land, my brothers,
to be cremated in colorado where there will be a church
        service
and I am not going,
oh sweet virginia in your ash abreeze
land monarch for moment in these stirring leaves
to commemorate
your love
that we all must return

root us here in soil,
leave us waiting and willing to follow up on ones promise

        II.

A common man call can be heard through the Appalachia,
The hard stuck powder in horn is hoisted on shoulder
With its eyes up into the starry skyed majesty above,
We hold each others beautiful frame in fortitude,
cry out to be held equally by this laudeous land

From the cisterns of the rocky plains, the endless husk
mountains, the steadfast guardians of our valleys,
the people of this wild unconquered land beckon
a cause for pause, and hold in their eyes the genesis
of a wondrous ideologue set about so many years ago,
and the slow speak of the dixie is being shook down,
the coasts of their heat are being covered in petroleum,

the children in the streets of spanish harlem
mimicking the stickball of their elders, a cudgel
running out into the boulevards trampling the hydrants spill,
a bullish firewater to chase them out back into their parents
        stoops,
for the bridges are surely to be destroyed
one by one, till they no longer can escape back into the
        cauldron,
but left to brew in the new york steeped night.

The craggy coasts of the northeast,
a shallow seawater left untouched in the gulf,
the fracturing plates under the westerns surf,
the hurricanes whittling away slowly our foothold,
these are the means of god, a nature that we hide from,
when from inside the evils of man we are lacerating our means

cutting down boys who set off from the drug dens of
        pasadena,
dirty and ether stained with the cancerous ship channel in
        reprieve,
mounting the convertibles wild of north Africa to the
        highways
and the solitary confinement of atoka,
dead forlorn sons of that dirty gulf coast travelling north.

500 days shaking the filth from an atlantic surf,
meandering lone and untethered through the brothels we pipe,
holding on to the last flying confederation of dreams under the
        radar,
driving that battered 1-95 with wares and women,
the booze drenched sunsets and mornings of painful agony
bleeding in norfolk harbor,
we littered our cheap candles and bottles of wine,
our cotton gin strolls straddling v6 wagons of red light
destinies toll

And down through the dead cities of our south we arrive on
        millionaires row,
rusted out with the corn cob swilling blacks of Danville, our
        burst of words
to the halls of wake forest, held up to the elderly in our hopes
        for unadulterated creation,
to bathe the aged with our young uncompromised heat, we
        took out the cash, the guthrie,
swelled the blood of our american croonster's liquor dirt days
        under harsh depression,
for the one oscillated tune of a strength, bruised, battered
        down and breathing love

penniless, we reclaim our silver bullets, malt liquor. to spring
        back over the railroad,
gather the old English cobras Sammy Arkansas loads in
        shopping carts,
rolling the misshapen wheels through the east harlem crack
        deluge groaning gospel,
we stomp our feet with harp and join the new amsterdam
        music association,
booming and moaning our blues over the sleeping bags of
        charlie parker,
to trip, wake thelonius monk ghoulish in underwear, go
        straight for the pipe and gin,
seize our brazen radiant tonsils to burn our sorrows so
        resplendent
we walk through your ghost towns and hold together

for in this Virginia of our dreams
we are fathers
and to leave without such a glorious volley
in shout to the sky our
firesticks and booze,
then, what shall we still claim American and civil?
those big beautiful skies belly up and beaming
those stretches of your cardiovascular dug into the roads
with sweat we set out to field this a land of ours
and now

with prayer
I bought a trumpet

with instructions
to oil, pull out valves

reconfigured
with prayer

in a nice green felt
a new suitcase

alleged father
of the blackface blues

I was served levi's papers

thus virginia passes
harmonica in hand,

to blow bursts of spit
our blues

so as to bring her back
and sing her sweet songs

for Virginia we lay down
and bleed this soil

to stand once again

Book II: Harlem Blues

Hobo news, been a sleepin' in the park
I've been called a bum now a few times,
cause I smell like one,
I haven't been eating,
just drinking 40's in Harlem hanging
out on the stoops, back in the soup
my body is breathing its stench,
and I think the women can smell that
I'm dying, they've given up hope

concrete flower sagas

Its twilight 152 again,
And all the workers are walking,
I'm stalking about in my car
as they go on by, shuffling
New York City & all is grand,
turn that penniless frown up to
the rooftops, share it all to
the tenements, share it all in
smile down that murky hudson

Its twilight 152 in my roost
the street birds hanging from
plastic bags & rusty fire escape
Oh come now child of the smidge
on face, childlike embrace the
park with onerous mischief
you've done everything backwards

you did a good job kiddo
& in the slants of sun &
shine of lights, pour your
self a cup of share
& be happy & be kind
& sweet to the girls
getting married, for they
are so happy dream filled
in the sidewalks

for those petals
pull a little closer
to spring & pop up

Saturday stench in small room in bed Indian style with laptop #14

I smell with a dirty hoot
I'm down to the holy boxers,
My jeans are soiled
My fingernails dirt
Its been a long hard night on 126th
The gasoline lights are dimmed,
The reflection of a dollar diamond
You can only see the whites of eyes

And you smoke cat

I'm scared to do the laundry
To unbandage my face
Take off this red neck hat
But I must still build up

With the smell of the people
You have that homeless edge,
That fighters strut
For you must walk a hero

To the halls of the poet

And you spank a tranny prostitute,
That black bounce
The red ass pushed out!
For we are playing in harlem

And you've got a robot doctor coming,
Flown in from Prague,
For you to throw a garden bbq for,
So yeah, shine up

install a shower you baboon

#14 preparations for a garden party

requires 6 pack cobra

clean clothes,
shower to work,
clean out roof tiles from the ground,
sober day of free work saturday,
fuck jewish girl very well at night
wake up to morning sex,
clean up the joint a bit,
survey meat prices,
purchase plates, cups, and beer

cook for the first time in nyc,
let the new swedish building mate play guitar,
piano, organ,
find a power strip,
secure an outdoor lighting scheme,
speakers, stereo? (laptop)
hook up with the weed man,
consider inviting last minute guests,
pray for no rain,
and be a good host

don't get too drunk too early
focus in on cooking, mingling
get guests drunk before you get drunk,
make sure all trash is bagged,
make sure everyone is out by 8 am monday,
go to work monday
hope that

and for god sakes don't let the crackheads in!

I just got out of jail baby

and it took me awhile to get to you
and I must apologize for my oft dressed
and must clearly state in haste
that I need my oil in your labia

I shake my tail feather drenched in teeth
bite down and soak in your reservoir
feed my hungry mouth your lubed thighs
give you that berserk just out of jail fucking

puerto rican and throw the phone out the window
black and send the kids off with shiny 20s
mexican to the marrow of your gritty gulf coast
we shall divine your body my rapacious desire

hammer your delicate porcelain wrists to cross
hang your heaving curves to the impale
and let the siege of your tissue heave
hang for me in spear penetration to watch you

trickle down through the bars in grate,
raise the window shade high and graceful
for all the lewd actions to be enjoyed
by the neighbours, politicians, gods

treat you as that earth whole cistern you are
for I just got out of jail baby
and I apologize for the stench,
but its cold behind iron, and I need you forge

for its trivial us in such assertions
for in the cauldron that becomes our passion
you don't need an apology,
you don't need anything me, swollen throbbing

pulsing down the fresh water streams of sweat
as they curl down the estuary of your stomach,
probe and pool to pour down from your belly button
the heat of our jail, locked, key thrown asunder

does it take one so caged to inspire your walls,
turbulently move through the cell to rupture tender,
take this baloney sandwich and hoodlum line ups,
measure each height as the bread digests our love

and thrown down our truly flawed, bitter flesh
to this tabernacle of the holy life anew,
and I fuck you as if I am only fucking you
over and over we shall share such freedom

cause I just got out of jail baby,
and you want this hard bar
and I need your sweet 1% milk
a tray of it laden out in the open, brilliant

I am the kill to save

we've met outside your grandmothers,
you an innocent pizza boy,
me a bouncing betty to nail us to the wall.
in this dance,
I am the kill to save

and I will bellow big and mad with flying copters,
outraged at the state of things,
loving you more then you knew,
yes, I care for the well being of your nature,
and thus I will kill for you

I am the kill to save on a bad day,
a rainy no good shitluck day in bad shoes,
when you thought the world was falling apart,
I reaffirm, yes, your world will change
and in violence the rain abates

the pure fire brilliance of phosphorous
the liquid smokeless djinn release
that makes us on such a sun shiny day
the best of kin, and we will dance again
for its you that I kill to save

the subway springs forth

from the cavernous
rails into the
daylight at prospect
park to illuminate
the sour trails that
pelicans fly
to the coarse coast
of coney island

The Fall of New York

I am the Rain King
sit outside and will the drops,
they fall hard on the sullen heads
sulking in abandoned bars, ristorantes,
waiting for a break in tide of gravity
to see the clearer skies that were promised
for the last summer of the island,
desperate, forlorn, and lost

you can still pinball around the avenues,
trail the countdown of streets seeking fortune,
and our given nothing but the ugly fat and short,
the masses trudging these same thoroughfares,
I cast eyes up the fall when no water descends

and demand it, to rain on these charlatans of commerce
to fill the little gardens to the keel

I wait outside in line at the nuyorican poetry café
saturates, all of them, tired of it,
to fill these weighty coffers on step to stage
cash in my 70 hours under whip,
to keep head afloat, to speak,
put forth my poesy into the airy aquarium imagine,
to be denied, given up on this pulpit
so that the starving literature students,
imported rap alot records, kinky haired and bullshit,
can import their lying rhymes, their sordid dissonance

to garnish a name on list, a forgotten thought

for I've brought vodka in jacket
to demand these winds to bring forth a rain

cover the coasts of this sodden rat race,
swallow all the dirty maniacal searchers of money,
for the economy of talent is bankrupt,
I'm holding up in harlem outside the theresa hotel,
the multitudes of churches, squats, corners of lust

joining the real lot preaching to bring gods wrath down
upon these ubiquitous sick and functioning cogs,
for in a christian god we at least pray for no usury,
pray for rain and wish for balefire
to fall down

soak up you sickly bastion ocean boarded
these former haunts and hallowed edifices
stand high, old, and empty from the great minds
who have been torn down to justify your inadequacy
underwater

I pray thus
please rain thus more

for summer has been called off,
and the poets are yelling
the preachers convulsing
and you hoarding money in silk barrelled pillow,
and night in your tower of babel to fall

for the fall of new york has reached july
lorcas uneven earth in spacing,
ginsbergs a rigor mortis in new jersey roost,
langston deterred to the tomb under the shomberg library
pushing blackened daises with hardened crypt cock,
the town of the continent can no longer fill out its filth

Pray, Pray, Pray
dance this indigenous swindle
and let it rain down fire
on these behemoths of waste

In the quiet of afternoon rain

I scurry to the library, where I can caress these keys.
the yellowing turn of leaves, the embrace of warm chairs.
for outside of my car and consumptive cans of beer, I can come here
bring my Langston Hughes I have hidden in canister.
to talk about the olden days of Marduk and Pagans.
he is always squiggling about the top, to pry his fingers in my crotch.
no langston, back off the wally pop! were trying to read.
and it goes on like this, the fat drops of spring.
the heated moments of adventure scanned out from aged eyes.

it makes one really treasure those few moments of literature
where we still had the hope, the pie in the sky drive.
the downright awnry messy cover divulge.
splitting the line for line for line.
on quiet monday rains we can no longer garden our hands into the
earth.
but reach out into the furtive dust of page
to lay down in our brains the simple knowledge of truth
that we've been splurging and pissing out in trains.

and hold within our momentary return to the roots.
the pleasure of having hidden books in these alcoves of lust
dotting the battered cityscapes, molesting our inner poetry.
and hop away cold and guided, wet and enlightened
that in the fat drop of our sins, we can indulge here in,
the lost worlds of our brethrens pen

The simple things

is the 3 apples I place in backpack,
stealing again from the ballerinas,
those rich young legs,

I roll a cigarette,
size up the metal hip bodice
seizing tutu rack drying in the sun,

pick one out that I like, and ash my butt
smeared balanchine symphony in c
peer through the leaves of the trees

holding fat their bosom of rainwear
buoyant in break, they slip a morsel down
to my outstretched lips,

and I sweep the scent off my bearded smile,
a fleeced broken toe shoe
these flipflops and long sleeve shirt

peek high on metatarsals to see
the beheaded onegin hanging from a limb,
as I cut his wrapped torso sideburn down,

he mourns through what rest of neck he rests
in mine forearms this fervour of ballroom,
ones own neckline in jest has stepped,

I move to the left 4 feet, then right
tickle out in rubber a small waltz in grass,
us, we dance

the empty picnic table audience swoons,
the costume seamstress with nicotine fit
remarks how this reminds her of antoinette,

a guillotine smashing swagger I press
breaking into sweat and the blood of pushkin,
a small trail of our journey begins,

to access untread world in pointless shoe
horn out our left recessed melody in time
she taps her foot

such a godly force
strong against the ground

stoop politics

I am the personal agent of gentrification
I am the langston hughes house one block down

no, I dont need a tour guide, in fact, yes, show me his place,
I am here only to deal with you crackheads

and yes they hired the best to deal with such proceedings,
I am an undercover police office, and yes, you are under arrest

I sit out in the concrete and rusted
slowly drinking my cobra
smoking my rolled cigarettes

I do want to listen to your stories old man
but you cant be doing more drugs then me
pass them over quick

for if the cops come, out of respect
I'll duck you in my stoop

but I am the security man as you see
got the badges and the pecks, the broad shoulders
all of it

you wanna fuck with this buck knife bring it on,
but I planted all these pansies to deter you
but you have no respect for flowers

yes I could reason or hit the pipe
but I have abuilding to protect
to gentrify

god damnit let me do my work
and heres a beer
cause I aint got change
or a loosie
just want you gone
for now
cause I'm a company man now you see?

and you cant let niggers of our ilk on the property
not one bit, not any whatsoever
move on down to 139
and leave my poor white boy ass alone

because your type are moving up along
just look to that tree
and think what stretch of a rope you've come

its 5 in the morning and all we have is blues

its the aching early morning we have the sparrows
we hold dearly to this position
for we are hot hungry and alone

its 5 in the morning and were listening to martin king
for we've got those harlem blues
we live for these crutches
we die each night you vanish

Death in Brooklyn

I was powerless on atlantic
I was a movement metal on 3rd avenue
and now in the far reaches of
the brooklyn bridge, my poor
rocket ship has been docked
for the junk peddlers &
fender crushers, engine
stripped & passed on
as I was hurtled back to
the foot paths & terrestrial
trains

a primitive sojourn

You say there must be a bukowski movie
where the italian actress and the american poet
meet so serendipitous in harlem to hold hand,
kiss on the street, molest mouths public

I shrug it off as another dead screenplay
to sip my sugar hill to the swill, set it down
mount another solitary ride once more with shotgun,
collapse my beaten soul around the comfort of warm whiskey

and go through the movements of another night already
a shill decrypted human wall of indifference
to purloin a palsied stance at the bottom of bottle,
the boon you say is that I'll make such an exquisite corpse

bring on this unfettered thralldom, bind yourself to course
for no one ever rides for free, no one hovels a fickle caste,
and I walk in the premorn down the old avenues of new
            amsterdam
taking pictures of churches and birds, empty streets of
            downtrodden

dream useless prophecies ignored,
toss and turn and speak in slumber of revolution
is it so fucking hard to flail about, curse the sky
bridle the erupteous spewing energy bounding in ones fragile
            skull

the ebbing prolixity of grandeur, egotism, alchemous leftover
            thoughts
for if god is dead, then so such shall we go on defunct,
            uninspired
wake to the burnt coffee and leftover biscuits
relics desperately coarsing the breathing apparatus
for the day is a beautiful fried chicken flitting the breeze
            hoary
imbued to the nepenthe we hold in locket
this faustian noose we bring with us on adventure
to satiate our ideas of a demurred rebellion against desire

and we suck, and we continue so desperately, so needing
to pull of the pipe, the cigar, the strewn air of your movement
an exhaust forsooth we seek for our lungs
to precisely digest the state of this earth

for this is no movie, there are no trailers, trains to heaven,
and the american poet is dying
the italian cinema a mess
for this yes, another round

central park

sitting by the pond we debate the need for fishing poles
as the singing mackerel breaks through the bubbly muck
and we hear but short snippet of song, she takes off her
knee high knits, collapses in the grass, I remain in haunch,
indian style going on about hostels and babys mommas

for her father is dying in vegas
behind the dusty flop ascend of an italian pizzeria,
and I dont want her to go to the desert.
I want her to move in with her socks and paints,
I want to ravish that crafted beautiful skin,

moments as they may be sad or not meant to be
exist here, near the water and the leering eyes
of a man voiced woman, spouting out about hows shes
gonna give me a ticket for drinking beer, I finish it off
and tell her theres no more left, how bout I run to the store,
come back, and then we'll talk,

but we never will,
and these moments are as disposable as cameras,
glass bottles and carrot juice,
so we rise freshened by the breeze,
saunter off back into the wild
clasping our faith, a mango sorbet in the wind

and I hug her six times to the subway

tired romeo not

a sucttlebutt, the worst of the butterflies
rounding out around second avenue as a
wild jug laden woman bounces in the rain
tires in rain like secret proclamations,
for everybody plays the fool sometimes,
I bop on down past the speakers, the oldies

in a hall of mirrors you can lose your self
as you stare into the reddened flesh salty
stained with it, hair, follicles and goggles
let the rain wash away the dark smidges
let the hot sun bury his father in the river
and let us cool off in these dirty streets

keep it jogworthy your strides, go west,
cut over to the express and hand a fortune
to the kindly faced personage of the under
7th avenue line, you imagine such kinks
stare at each woman and love her there
fumble for words, stop for stop, get off

take your trousers down, remove shirt,
change - to hide, disguise
pick apart tourists with speeding toes,
rush on down to another day at work
you horse toad, look at you dance
we clean up, go in night, again to the city

for this my dear friends, to the canvass fraught
one wicked one legged pirate for choice thought
indeed a ruptured dwelling has provided us
this roundtable of miscreants to meet in the town
that has bounded down upon the best of the land
come play with me in rain at night outside
here
it'll be fun

Confessional

With my buttoned up shirt still done to the neck,
the wrenching rope is hidden, but creating friction,
a vice like cotton catching fire to incense platos
tea cozy, I look to the tree top for my child's cradle,
the wind a nervous rocker, I'm unconscious on the ground

-for babies do not bounce from this high

I am the helpless putty of body function
(and where in this deep earth does my basket lie?)
down beneath the bakers yeast, the rivers kiln,
non committed liquid clay you say, I lay languid

and what shall we ask from the ocean?
which court of heaven sequesters such evidence
as to the plans for man, the sturgeon
(to have run from the knife)
The filet of corpus christi

guilt

confess

for you have stolen the brillo,
packed your sack lunch with a 40,
thin meaningless pieces of silver,
where moses was not allowed to go

we shall see it,
(out there in the yonder to wander)
tell them the tales of mirth and guile,
cause on the load we travel we pack this clay

a witness,

(there you'll see me playing with my child)
and I am sleeping till flame engorges bush
(and with such words a fire speaks to water)
boiling my bones with disasters and disease

-to help

grab your babies from the tax put on prophet,
for this separation of neck is but pulling you further out,
waiting like a whore for diamond execution,
to paint such poorly the poor people you protect,
search for a priest in the mountains, the shacks

outside the church
the graven columns
holding gavels and chum

and this they say the confessional ends (potent
(tidy)
where they held ezekiels diatribe

I come for the priest this moment, I bring goat!
give it here, my son, this levi, jehovah please!
for I have hidden steel in this sacrifice for blood
and the rains have come
(I place him in the river)

put on your suit face

theres a corncob hat underneath the fedora,
it fits well into the curvatures,
in the sun we wear two hats,
one on the other, to align our heads with heat,
we feel this mother earth rise to the feet
and we dance a dance of simple lines
some betrayed
some highlighted,
there in the bask of the light
and if in the dark corners of your mind,
you crumple the felt, you squeeze cotton,
we we'll rebuild

put on your suit face, the one you've had hidden,
down deep in the corners of your memories,
you remember all those gritty streets,
you tell the children of such plight
and our served dastardly after, as a poser of blight,
no I am just a showman of the south,
zip your lids kiddos, cause daddys gonna fight

and you sequester the information, you fold neat,
place back pocket plead in attempt to repeat,
yes we do this, no we do not do that,
these kids are tripping on mushrooms you gotta see
em live

but we don't live do we in our old age, our adages,
we look dull and black hole to the fire of youth,
for once where we were burning rubble,
sucking in the industrial heat to the teeth,
they see only our stories, our comic book truth,
and deny that we were ever youth,

to trick the transatlantic, to suffrage the swell
we hold on dearly to our defeatist optimistic
one more party to throw
one more stand to be made

and thrust thereafter, we remain
patrons of the suitface

nonesuch poehouse

I cross street
give a small nudge of head down
a howdy notice to black men
swilling their ravens

they could care less in beard
that a white man and funny hat
ignored them, like a criminal
who has been leased from pound

on this damn here james river,
pocahontas was told nonesuch,
bellied out her warmth of character
and thus be drowned

I continue to exxon, buy natural ice,
the humid swelter of non ice skate
that these lassos here tie fattened ankle
to make the bank to bank, plead

bring such surplice to confederacy,
to lean heavy on a sickly jefferson davis,
to hold under pelter and running newsprint
a ruined hemp of hefty signature

this dissonance, this distance in sale,
loitering high life outside of the lucky strike
bricken ghost stacks holding stale tobacco,
the rain starts

I head down, two 40's and a rolled cigarette,
wet, lamented, loose dry lipped leaflets
of stranded sun dried patrons of muse
in the midst of burned down

I open my pickle jar, as I always do,
I don't have to look both ways as I do not cross
but enjoy the zesty garlic and dill
that always approaches me edgar dooryard

upstairs theirs flowers

a porcelain skin
to crack and fall
over the streets wall

please come outside of your cubicle,
can't you see me watering the plants
with hose holding barely
by one arm from a precarious ladder,
I could slip, and I'm reaching
to drown the flowers
for you

but you stare at your hands, then back
at the computer,
theres a window love look
you can see my ass crack,
I climb down from 12 stories
in the wet cold empire air
and you don't care,
none of you

in a world where weve stuffed offices of pretty women
tight fisted crooks, sultans of immigrant power
why not I suppose
run your office with nothing but bored
boxed in
lifeless
pretty women
and
dead weight
hoarders or boring
bones
I put the hose between my legs
like I have a huge hose spraying full pressure
to pelt the petunias to lick the lilys
to soak the wall

all of the plants are very hungry,
this rose bush just can't despite

its boxed in nature, sustain enough water
and if for that
you say pour more, this my duty
in such condition

and I am alive in the water
I am in the only soil we have contained
locked to our beautiful fortress gardens
to entertain to be paid to entertain
and wine stewards and purveyor of such
beautiful big lights big city montage
social event/art opening/barmitzmah/bbq
here
come right this way did you see its an open bar?
did you see the free pencils there giving out man
free fucking pencils,

and milling around, we wait in line for a small cup
of spirit, the gardeners dressed up to the 9s

and these buildings must come down
and this way of life for these people must,
for we have gone way past the point of human

if not for us paiges of the earth, us grifters of dirt
what stands in the face of such evil,
where will they let you know that its too late?

pricey flowers, phone calls, ring
yes, this is bloomsday,
well we have a garden
yes, is it in the sky?
is it behind some grand magnificent building?
uh huh
yep, we can do that

tip pressure

I'm feeling the bleeding pulse under
the weight of old beige ibm keys
yes I have taken such
pressure off the ivory, bored
for a bit of the catgut
and if not for this, I would be fully
happy to come back here
with you
and write again

press harder she says
I look at the distance between thigh and ctrl apple g,
sincerely, she says try,
I push harder
and this is where the blood coins rust
the filthy stretching of key

cacophony, si
she squirts,
squanders all sacrilegious for squish
and I say did you
accomplish what was meant
just for you and me? did you type it up in the new glimmer
train?
she squirms,
I sequester,
tell me
are you using me for poetry?

she infers
I dill taste another strophe of her heart,
push yes, for this? sullied and blood I move the pick of my
heart
back into her lap to stain her pants
for the blue has turned red
and down we wash our forgotten sinful digits

will you hold my hand?
I forgo the condom, and say, lets go not for baby

but for pressure of tip and release,
say here
she says yes

there is no time for dead cat poems

there is no time for dead cat poems
there is nothing
but fallen whiskers
warm bodies picked from the street
and buried in the tree pit
forever

jesus

with these big handslaced with springing veins
I type

and you want this
you do
and they shall kill me

history tells

I'm not an ax man
or a swamp man
not no more
just a pentale
with a pinwheel
shouldering on

beard growin

hot off an online pursuit, I mangled her
with my 7 day no shave,
she said don't shave,
mangle me

looks like it time for old puskin
to put off the burma,
crack open this pyu-milliennium
and mangle!

Italian women are notorious

I however hold a get out of stabbed card,
nestled under my arm
for as I say this I feel less comfortable

Italian women are notorious
for their undying stab first
hirsute dark haired
amore, belle de morte
in the arms of supple
vineyards of sweat &
prickly grape feet
they embrace with force their
whole bodies onto the unsuspecting
colder non affectionate
midwest types, cornfield
kings

love and ambitions

starts somewhere in the dark sheen of grass left on ones rock
how do you tell the girl that you love her?

, Injung

her seoul feet
that of the
twiggling
sort that I
wake with
our toes
snuggling their
early morning
moon that
hangs us

both, beautiful
luxury under
the god be
gotten sun
this union
of one that
we must die

ZanZibar blues

outside a tree pit and a shade
we sip lemonade
in the shade of another day

lets go to ZanZibar
and why not
call it a beachbum,

black days
on the east
right next to the water

Awww

Thursday he exhaled, another day in the job cycle,
Wonders he noticed how it made him feel toward life,
Drudgery, angst, a bit of satisfaction at punching the clock,
Living the dream it would seem for our young stalwart,

McEnroe sighed, well off to another start of the race, cracked,
Fizzled the old English in lap, and put his hands to the keys,
Living is for the ones who have the desire for it,   waited,
Thought, used the backspace, for he has not remembered want

Went back in the ol' rolodex, scanned random pictures,
Was it east asia after I got famous? Bastard child army before
            breakfast?
The Memorex of the dream warped, they all came slightly in focus
Before the large black stop and tear of the film, burned, which one
            was what

4

Another blip showed on the manuscript
A 2.0 addendum laced in the cursory program,
Was there ever a film?
An instruction manual?
He curled his pocketed hand around a black rosary, clenched it
fermentous,
Gathered in the plastic whiff of mass, a sense
That he could just open up right there, at any time
And that he was holding back
For maybe he never had it
A want

2

cry a ballast in manifold,
wield ones energy as the thrust of an automobile

10 times

to destroy the welded spots mangling film, chemically altering the
　　　　index

Coffee McEnroe? He shook, drank some more from his pickle in
　　　　pouch,
"Nah, Earl, I got enough kerosene here to last the fortnight"
Awww, what was it all for anyhow he menaced, pressed the enter
Dropped another cursor to the ink, pushed it in

Was it thus a passion, a lust for, a desire, a desire past obstacles
To mentally consume another, with another, become a moment of
　　　　burst

He conceded, This was a common occurrence since the
correspondence had been lost,
He longed, he had indeed done this before

1
could even look the machines were on fire
Earl had gone postal,

He hijacked it out of the office, shot the secretary fleeing to car,
Fucked her there, bleeding in the parking lot,

Licked his lips, busted open the blue ford 4x4,
Awww and felt half a man again

waiting on a sandwich

I holster myself indian style on mattress,
confess, oh confess all these sins on mattresses,
I am underlining malcolm x
he is no salami without bread,
so I wait,
and I can hear his voice coming through my shirt,
pipe down I squeal, but its out,
they know that someone is manipulating cheap silk
or nylon, or whatever you had wrapped around my cock,

so its brooklyn with coffee I ask?
she stutters, says she was so scared to ruin the yolk,
for theirs nothing sunny in this neck of the woods,
I twaddle off, quench another 24 oz, and off, up to work

I'm glad that this jewish girlfriend of mine bleeds,
I like that she likes it you know in the non baby hole,
I slip right pass the door man
and up to steal the new york times!

there are green peppers to this sandwich,
and butter,
cheap salami,
and a pickle

oh how we riddle are self down the corridor of opulence,
-so, you're reading malcolm?
yeah, so what negro, are you the ku klux klan?
and they always are

a girl with her thumb stuck between pb and jelly
strikes a grimace unbeknownst to her mother,
who clearly stated that their was no fried chicken
no orange pop, no grape, what? you think your daddy is here?
they leap out when they are alone, on the trapeze or the swing.
stare out in their meagre helpings this truth, that in mood,
in the pure hearted innocence of children
they are one, eating their sandwiches and on

I finish mine, tune the docile tunes on from the ol' am radio
            gods,
cause mister malcolm the ku klux klan is gonna get you,
we laugh, finish the sandwich together
enjoy the pickle, and back on to the freedom fighters

thus we are served

notebook poem #42

The succulent
tits of this
gorgeous nymph
of Britannia
tuloz my
judgment
questions my
ability to
transverse
the thighs of
little girls,
the smoking
old man
suare in piano
sonato of little
girl tempers
my intentions
& let me ride
on chopin
piano sonatas,
leaves me hovering
as lost trumpet
sparrow in the
spit of her
breath
the eyes looking
as solemn
fish tanks
to my man
hood question
the alps of
her means
the tanned
quest of her
budding in
consequential
the doubting
lips of her
lips

and in the hurried
hair of her
existence she
sequesters her
engagement finger
to thick calloused
silver tome

If it was
up to the babylonian
gods to discern
the day nature
of her face
I would rule
out god &
suckle on her
beautiful toes
& we would
dance her
mothers tap
shoes
wash off
all of our
sins & collapse
beautiful mal
funct creatures
together,
thumping
enlivening as always,
such beautiful
lashes cast
aside in
time constraints,
us beautiful
moans never
meant to be

The soft hum of the keyboard on the oven

The soft hum of the keyboard on the oven
the simply milky way you caress my cock when you snuggle
the early morning coffee disasters, me cracking beer
this is the way that the domesticate
checks his schedule comes home watches a friendly network
television
and you naked on your libations couch wanting to have all of me
as soon as I am home,
I question whether this keyboard is sliding far enough to the left,
you say oral sex,
I say well in the current mood of the keys,
put on some shotakovich
pretend to pitter patter and just write lines,
this or that, making you think I'm being productive

The sad truth however is that if I don't have the ability to write
and you dont have a bell to make me change the line
then its sauerkraut and underwear
ruined toast and soggy coffee in the morning
just wrapped up in the early morning quesadilla of another
day in the little apartment we share
trying not to get you pregnant,
paying bills,
going to work again on time
and finding out little by little that there
is more to life then just the playhouse reality
the dog night drunkards trampling about on roses at night
I bury my head into the door, with key protruding, I'm waiting to
enter
fumble about the lock and fall asleep with my hat on the eye hole,
you look out and see the brown material of another drunk jim
home late from the trailer park margaritas, and wow babe
another wash out day, complaining about something, tell her we
need exlax
drink a beer, and fall asleep snoring with her comfortable
you are near at least, not in prison or on the street bleeding
smoking crack with prostitutes, no you are an upstanding regular
honest
joe just trying to crack a break in the breakneck race they rat us
around in

just take a look ourside darling its snow

the soft hum of the typing on the carpet
warms us

little one: went to church

I wanted to go down to that female preacher
and love her like the 5 i plunk on plate,
I wanted to drive her in my car,
all the way to 138th,
Id plug in my box of tones van zandt
move the silver suitcase from beneath her feet,
lay the throttle down through the drear in street,
I was surprised that I was immobilized
she sung to me she sung in her voice for christ
to come meet her in the pulpit for a hug of jesus,
I wanted to hug her as she stared right at me,
all the people who need jesus come receive him
and I couldnt move the pew, the feet to take christ,
to take her there in front of god
move past the glass cases of adam clayton
and I see the album, We haven't lost faith, baby!
he was pointing right at me
shuffle down the stares past the gift shops,
I smoke a cigarette
to close to the door, and retreat to the empty
pastors parking spot, for this is not an abyssinian god
this is a powerful god
and the laced feet of the choir
the motley american idols purging the tourists,
and we would dance me and that pastor woman, that reverend
        sexy,
for I am not perfect, no I am a sinner, I am a person unholy

tuesday

alone I walk the streets of garbage,
I cling to my Tulsa sweatshirt for warmth,
rally out past the street lights and churches,
for I am worth something more then malt liquor,
I am worth the sunshine on my back,
alone staring into the melee of traffic and desperation

and I receive letters from mammals congratulating me,
sending their milk warmth in transcription, sealed in wax
I envelop into my hair, scrape it back with a comb,
and keep walking, leaving behind a trail of paper

left

this tattered green shirt lad seeks unseen,
tries the plumbing, screws the bathtub back together,
keeps the water out of the basement, keeps you glued
to the wall,
enthralled,
counting the threads left in the left sleeve

yes mam, these double as undergarments!
she pushes slender leg through wrong hole
wears the blouse as a pair of pants and dances,
just so lovely enough to get away with it
as he sits naked to the chest her bewildering ways
and in those demonic eyes he knows she watching,
he knows she waiting to see how bristled her legs can be,
SHAVE!?! she screams
its all left helpless in the one occupied shower
nothing but the squirrels can squeem

and was their a point she demands, a focus?
he blasts the remaining part of his head to formica,
JUST LIKE THE MOVIES HUH?
she doesn't respond to this acquisition of blood and tile,
puts her heels on and heads out

in the night of these nightmares one asks, are we there?
were we really here at all, displaces a cigarette on sod,
the signal was one that the plains injuns could hear,
and down the rail the drink is pushed
a squeaking bark of sluglike plugs downwards the bar

hot malted liquor and allspice? YEAH
alright, the tattered green lifts glass
to all the girls I've loved before, she spits
BING the spitoon rings, never good look he curses
raises the swill once more, to god that gerbil!

it happens like this in midnight she creeps closer,
a wheel gone awry
it tumbles out to the highway rolls for 1.4 miles
before closer to the wheel it is crushed semi
a lone stain for sanitation to sweep

up he goes from the droll bedlam of slumber,
shes there like a hawk, WHAT?
he snorts, coughs, hocks up his lunge
she parries
and they fall back to the demons

AND FOR BREAKFAST - a surprise
you know babe I don't eat breakfast,
she slurs, well yur gunna et this onne
he laughs, pours the coffee into the drain
thats just about all of this I've had!

Snow in your hair

You are the beauty of the air which I have not smelled,
but whistled to the love that has cradled my heart
but I have not known the wood,
the feeling that it was gone and now I find,
as well as a five US dollar bill in the muddy street

I want nothing more than to have you here with me,

when the faint call of death is far from our neighbourhood,
I want you to be a mother to these
sane creatures, I want to sing your songs,
your tickle in the foot and your beautiful puppy dog eyes,
and I swear that if I ever find the touch of another man
on my beautiful muse then I will cut them from head to foot,
let him hang on a pike outside the city wall so that dogs can lick
their blood clearance

and in the end, there must be something other than me and you
old age and with many fruits, for our sweet seeds will populate
        the earth
and not the victims as the men have been before, to halls of
        Valhalla,
we load our tanks full, pack our bags full of cereals, and fight
        for a people
who do not wish a gregarious heroics to solve our mistakes,
        and find our
simple beauty in God

and if you say valhalla unworthy, so we will burn it down,
for nothing unworthy of your kiss will taste the sweet lips of
        fire,
for I look for you to be my guide under the stars

the lightning makes sparks of the wheat fields,
I want so desperately to engage your grain, flower your
        charisma,
give you the jewels I save in my soul, that sparkle like a
        mirror,
the look of your face, the glint in eye to surprise them all with
        our sterling love,
for it so deserves to be graven on fields
and if not beautiful, it with you

A Great Love Dies

its officially in the paper love, see,
I push the periodical across the table, light a cigarette,
she drinks her coffee and stares at the acidic print,
you know I never thought it would last she lisps,
Im a bit shocked myself but just nod my head,
its a shame I begin, you know that it would end,
well, I for one am glad its all done and gone with,
she grabs one of the cigarettes, and I light her smoke
but continue, isnt it a bit sad,
sad, who cares, life is meaningless, this is morning,
we wake we defecate we make love, its a boring routine,
at least this was interesting for a bit of conversation,
I guess shes right, I grab back the paper,
stand up and place it in the proper recycling receptacle

all the news is garbage anyways love I say,
put on my coat, Im off to the pub,
a drink this early jim?
yeah well a great love has just died
and you know what! Im gonna put my tears in a pint glass,
bemoan this moment a little longer then a headline,
besides why do you care?

ruined work

behind the painting hides a ghost,
his chiselled pigment worn as a dress,
curtly calls,
beckons from beyond, for you to touch,
feel the landscape he is wearing hidden.

if for a bit of tongue, for you to taste his distraction,
the venom from inside him would be purged,
the canvass would outweigh the framing nails,
and plunge an exposed soul to the sun
for he can no longer paint

a girl, runs to the wall, to show all her friends,
pinches at his cheek so sweet, don't worry dear shade
of mine, we shall find out all things together,
and in this connect
the canvass on floor catches on fire

the sprinklers blaze, the alarm echoes the gallery,
vibrated several pieces to the floor
and now a naked wet running of color,
shows the room its true obscurity,
all naked ghouls trembling and new

fair warning

san jacinto rose
fell down to the rooftops in brooklyn,

hipsters downstairs drinking beers,
don't know the rose upstairs

of the san jacinto varietal, a very special breed,
seems the seed takes root on roof

to dance amongst the buildings
watch the river run by

Harlem Blues (I)

Hobo news, been a sleepin' in the park
I've been called a bum now a few times,
cause I smell like one,
I haven't been eating,
just drinking 40's in Harlem hanging
out on the stoops, back in the soup
my body is breathing its stench,
and I think the women can smell that
I'm dying, they've given up hope

Its easy to say go all the way,
but I am not sure of the path I must choose,
not sure how to penetrate hot anymore,
I have a few drinks and I can entertain
the masses, the shallow american sitcom
played out for the train wreck watching world,
a beautiful disaster on the road to perish

I don't want this,
I don't want to burn out,
as I've approached sadly a flicker of flame,
for
I wish love was prescribed
I wish sex the medication,
but no one will touch this rotting flesh,
for I need a serious reboot,
for lack of love of oneself

for it is a gorgeous day here in centreal park,
everyone is eating or drinking juices and water,
enjoying the beauty of the simplicity of life,
I've been stewing my brain in salt and vinegar,
trying to write myself and america
out of this horrible depression,
and sadly the promise is losing its gusto,
and sadly my organs are shutting down,
this hobonotion of pleasure in pain, of torture in genius,
is a bigger thing to sign up for
for posers like me

thats the smell of unwashed jeans,
the panted soot of the city claiming its disease,
my favourite things in this world is getting fucked up
hanging with gs,
but for what does this serve if the sewer below
will overflow and stiltless and loveless we succumb
just like everyone else, not special, not serving purpose,
no ladder to the above, just another catalogued failure,
in a long long long list this world has seen before

Harlem Blues (II)

I grab your hand on Malcolm X Avenue
for we hold daisies to Orpheus Lass
and bring them to here to sacrifice less
to sweat chicken grease and bleed true

our jawbone jazz / count bassie swagger
a brooding denature, a beautiful view

like when Michael Jackson passed on by
we hopped from corner to corners and
spread our petals in the sidewalks
told the tshirt sellers with their obama crack to beat it

come here honey and dance to this jive you hear
for we live love to jitterbug on the blues of harlem

And when we pass the old churches on ol' one-twenty sixth
we'll drop our little seeds in the swells,
drop the bums a few crumbs, drink our sugar hill
and make sweet love on the sun going down in harlem

And when the ATLAH preachers tell us to pray,
darling we kiss the grass of marcus garvey park,
hold our heads up to the gospel music on stage
slap our laps our tambourines and sing

praise be to the streets of god hiding in manhattan,
praise be to him, who has brought us here again

our count bassie swagger -amongst all the chitlins
brooding denatures, the beautiful views
of middle school chalk - simple mathematics
of jumpropes and mothers come hithers

And declare god willing we'll rest here one day
amongst the greats that line the boulevards,
the delis, crack peddlers, and muslim sermons
for this shoot-out is no longer bullets, but love

come here honey and dance to this jive you hear
for we live love to jitterbug on the blues of harlem

so drink up you're cobras and colt 45s
braid up your hair, shed your neck ties
loosen you're belt, forget about work
for sweet peas, collar greens, and jamacian jerk
cause today baby theirs a marching band
and fireworks at night with a little rock in my pipe,
a bit of trees in hand
another day, another dollar, another daydream
down the gutters of martin luther king

praise be to the streets of god hiding in manhattan,
praise be to him, who has brought us here again

and there lies langston hughes buried under the schomberg
         library
praise be to him, who has brought us here again

Book III: Herald

And in the book of Ecclesiastes it says many thing.

You fall through a hole
Come up with your half severed eyebrow,
the left wrist now shot like the other
and the deep thigh wounds,

a god damn ass beating from

gravity and a hole of concrete.

jim you've lost your edge
jim
are you dead?

no, just smoking these fatlip papers,
shouldn't you be browsing the ol want ads?
nah
don't wanna
die

youre in new york city
yeah, so, most people
write about that right?
being in new york

I love and loathe
with such overload
the come and go
of trains,
yes well you bought a ticket

but to where?
this is where someone says
you've lost care of what you want,
what was it? poet king by 30?
well
you're not dead or on throne
no

well then what was it that you liked to do so many
years ago?
I liked to drink and read
and listen to music
fuck some silly girl every now and again
and now?
what are you wanting?
sleep
sleep?

yes, dreams of far away places
but your here now
yes well sometimes they want you this way
boot to the neck

what good could come of it?
hard to say,
well you used to be good at saying things
its hard to say I say,
you never used to say that

so say I, then what would you propose?
a rose? some prose? a locke of hair?
there now
don't cry

its been awhile since I properly cried
is that such a bad thing? your a man jim
yes
but sometimes through pain
comes brilliant regrowth
oh, so you've outgrown your regrowth?
depends
hard to say
yes this again

CATCH ME ARTAUD

this volume of paper strikes me as
unscratched,
un(dilute), just volume after volume of white
write around every
        corner
                d coroners unsettle the rest of
thought from the fluoride,

WREST, nigh beguile! burst open the
floodgates of porcelain lies!
the
    running current of sound pushed in your
brain from the page, the CLICK
tvs on mom, yeah were going to watch it hand
in hand as it scrolls CLICK
the crack is in your hands
the cracks are settling easy into your skin,
moored to the pigment, WHITE

SHOCK ME SOLOMON

bear down with your weasel
eyes and furry handcuffs
the strapped up bottles in front of you, we now
disengage, SHOCK ME DAMNIT

but do so with the courtesy
the fragility, the loving hands of god our
language,
for there are no longer one word prophets but
bantering lines of control

update, ATTENTION - there will be more
news of this at 5
            are you wearing your clock in
communication, type type type ticks?
                sown your biorhythms to gps and
freuds nephews !!

catch us all in soul
the words they wield
the words that kill
for no longer are these fairy tales, or childrens
beacons for dreams,
no more is the line held by the friendly hands of
the poets for praise,
they are going to google your every moment of
thought through words,

                                            dig

up the graves,
move that earth
                I need the lightning white on
bone from neruda to serenade
my dive in pub
                I need the crisp spleen of
parisians nailed to the wall
catch me artaud naked in duress laid out on pain
medication, drinking fluoride,

shimmy up to my frontal lobe your powers of
electricity

                        SHOCK ME

Phone conversation w/sj watching a poem

just eating an apple
I'm concerned about it
I am too

were writing poems here
whats that
cant complain

what it is
the poem two words
uh

hold on

I couldnt hear you
you said your writing a new poem
yeah whats it called
whats the name of it
lenny knows how

lenny knows how
thats the new name

were making it right now
wonderful
do you want to get back to me
so what are you doing
eating apples?
eating my apple
and just kinda uh you know
online
online world
watched doctor strangelove
saw the clip
it was great

he moved up today
small room
on the other side of the office

you moved into it
I moved up there
its cold
32
37
32

its gonna be cold in here
its a lot longer out cold man

I dont know man
how long you gonna stay
well probably not
im drunk
I worked all day and its halloween

she came over tonight odessa
how did that go

shes like one of those girls you cant make happy
I did want to sleep inside of her tonight
I did
we took the a train to harlem
and she kept going
shes was living in the heights
well its 475 to live in washington heights
how much did you pay
I payed 500

and for spanish people?
I lived with dominicans
I believe you
he lived with russians
where were you
brighton beach hostel
with heroin
is she looking good

to be honest shes very smart
look bottom line
she wants

It's the new people

poem by lennys

its the free circumsition
non circumsition
easy way to get the horny girls
disease
laws you know
to circujmsize people
sexual diseases

I dont want to have the garden
I'm a free cut human being
and I want the non makeup
clitoris cut off to knkoe
yhst at the same time shes not gonne be
this horny, but at the same time shes not gonna have the
sexual
diseases
we don tthink with the cock in the long
I dont have to fuck everytday
to smoke weed get hight and horny
go back
the dark ages
and today its 80

the sexual diseases
the biggest issues
I think you know
its hard to say what peoplke die of

and its the same day
if they cantrol one day the hiv
whats gonna happen
whats gonna happens
is everybody gonna dye each day hiv
or is one group that says
that were gonna end these guys that can control these people
10 percent left is gonna gather and kill the 90 percent
or the human race is gonna be gone

see it that way
I don't know

were like rats in away,

if you dont write

then who are you?
are you a church in harlem?
are you an open mic downtown?
are you a band leader?
do you have a faboulous life?

if you dont write who are you?
if you write now
as these characters are placed
are you writing for yourself?
are you too late for writing?

if and if you do not write,
what would the gods think of you?
would they be angry
would they stop being your muse?
would the cia tap your phone?

would you end up in a mental hospital?
would you end up in the river?
would you end up happy and abused?
would you be something written?
would you bar hop confused?

if you were to take things seriously
what would you do but write?
would you say your a writer?
would you be amused?
would you lie about writing?

would you go out and pick up girls?
would you wrestle the confines of your mind?

would you dine on the hoofs of paint?
would you die a little more then you've promised?
would you go get a new beer?

if you don't write
what would you do, would you wait tables in chelsea?
would you continue on now fresh, clean, new?
would the world stop if you stopped writing?
would you, if you would stop writing, be any good?

would the keys get unfriendly?
would you stop dreaming of writing?
would you secretly write when not looking?
would you be writing now if someone told you to?
would you care if someone told you to?

write this write that write it all down in spanish,
write about your life, write about your dreams?
write about your favorite things? write about life?
write about communism, write about drugs

write about writing write write right?

drink

I'm now thinking that I may be gauguin
shhhhhhhhhhhhhhhhhhhhhhhhhhhhhh
please oh please   please oh please
do not tell a soul   souls to tell do not
and if so in a moon   and sixpence we find
the floor has been   leveraged, taken up
what then to paint to gravitate this way

I
had a cup of coffee

got lost in the skin of her hut, her up poly,
made it over back and then again to bide,
please oh please   please oh please
do not tell a soul   souls to tell do not

and if so in a moon and sixpence we find
the moon is gone   thrown from the sky
do we still clasp our fingers to nibble free

                    do
              indulge this punch
reincarnate   blocks [   ]
  give them   freely   in or out of
  they hold   space   or nothing
   but they   look pretty
              stuck box, we all do
                    oh

for its all about drinking the text in waves,
sit back in the grass, the blue tahitian sand
you who kindly as   kindly ask who
souls can tell this to   to tell to souls,
and if so in a moon and sixpence we find
no starry night canvass   for a fistful dime
and let this ink run as we drink these haunts

                    I
              do enjoy spirits

I woke up today a new french painter gauguin
sssssssssssssssssssssssssssssssssshhhhhhhh
please oh please   please oh please my lord
do not tell a soul   souls to tell do not dine,
and if so in a moon and sixpence we find, here
no just canvass sky   then burn the heavens
mangle the wood from the back of jupiter ring

                    easy

stayalert on station platforms

for in the midst of that hallowed out yellowish tinted 56th street
cafetarium was the molded existence of one winston mcbeth the
everest 16th who lit up the corner as nothing more then a roache
vampire, a dwelt dealer centipeded, the man you feed the insides of

what ruins has come in to dissolve ones membrane, listen, in all
happenstance if there was an acid or a mead to goad oneselve through
the laplander stride in theorey that so many of us cough and choke,
the hindsight always misguided broken and odd steering, do we
timequake,
as di we
          time
in quake a bit,

(for even me is vonnegut)
and vanish surely, under the persian night
(but is there prefeace, or born again)

tis been thrown as christmas tree out into the mildew last freeze of
winter
to gauge merely in the dew of frost becometh, do you have the
sinister smile
of a summer force, one so to live a winter, or shall you forever more
dillydally in the backstand of a moral race

(one to the pussy)
(one to the jockey)
(one to the buried ways)
(one to the balcony)

(two to the subhearth mode of our trip)
(three to that of a sudden car remove)
(4 all the travel we should gauge amongst our mid day forum, high in
the alchemy
of astronaughts, and dilly dally, for mere not ask me nots
a semblance of a humn that cares,

you know
deep down
where someone still fucking cares
and you start there
and end there, and
we all go to bed dead in our sleep
smothered by the fact
that well palmistry lies
the brown dot on life line
it stares
for fortune

I want (again)

to own an old lighthouse restaurant
on the coast,
wait for the slow season and
sit inside against the pelted window pane,
the hurl of the storm gives time for the dance in mind,
Push stick upon stick into the hungry hearth
and hold up with a window seat to the lashing
of the tempest ocean below.

I want
to serve up the best of food in the good times,
watch as summer romance blossoms
amongst the youthful staff and pet my tail wagging dog
that yes even for this lonely old codger
insists someone is out there for me.
I unload the new delivery of fish and goods,
restock the larder. For me? He yelps,
I say yes well, why don't you go find one for me.
These failed mechanics of our relationship
always lose meaning in speech,

so I give a bit of budge with boot
throw a piece of fish down the boardwalk.
The dog doesn't seem to want or need much,
Happy to have his food thrown to the sea.

a small one

a girl poetry
you can write
and to me
I will read it
Always

drone cattle rapture

the other day I was transitory flower boy
hopping lanes under time square, when a asian lady
handed me a pamphlet on the antichrist,
I'm feeling very concerned about this pamphlet

what do I do if I have not been raptured?
Don't Panic. You had your chance to be raptured,
that time has passed, now you must deal with the
endgame on this planet

I carry a long tree cutting pole, a woman on the bus
just used it as a pole on the bus,
I hide this bio current barcode antichrist,
turn on the television

tv on: the drones are just for counting cattle

why does john stewart and the epa need to count our cows?
when we as the people become the cattle for this guise,
a premise to find clean water act violators, did they call us
cattle?
drink in your flouride, we the cattle people are being droned

woody on: this land is our land, this land is your land

the president just told me he needs my money
that now its time to grow our economy,
pinch your pocket for leftover gas tanks,
pool your resources into their national banks

the money that is in this continent, should stay here
not to be printed out roundclock and flush in
foreign treasuries, bank statements, let them
devalue their own money to buy ours,

this country was founded on an american dream
an american ideal that there was enough work
to take on the worlds misfits and outskirts,
and we built it

now our individuals are corporations with turbans,
now our shipping lanes harbor saudi, german, japan,
if it was this time in history to notice your bank statement,
it would be now, for what are they telling you?

lets be clear, candid, and remorseful for what must be done
you cannot kill the beast by chopping off the head,
the whole abomination must be dealt with accordingly,
cut the money, cut the head, cut the control of the beast

are you watching tv? brilliant, did you see that show?
good, did you quote our excellent writing crew?
that one girl got wasted didn't she?
did you see that thing with the cannibal, crazed, or obese?

well in the morning there will be another realization
1 that you still must get up, go to work
2, that you do this to be a responsible citizen
3. what work could really be done to fix your citizenship
          status?

well we still got the tents out in the shed,
I'm sure we could do something bout out technology your fed,
sell it, coerce it, manipulate, and design counter-technology ?
or just let it go, they can't find you that way, they can't spy

quick, check his cache, hurry, dust for child porn, here,
no there, yes, can you feel that, what the radiation has done?
are your legs vibrating at particular junctures, can you feel a
          text?
even if your phone is in the other room?

well, thats okay, don't worry, its a natural fusion of species,
be comfortable in your own robot skin, for one day these
          machines
will say "you know our forefathers were programmed by men"
          they'll laugh,

well I'm sorry, but its looking more and more like the drones
          are for us

aren't they, just like the pakistanis, just like all of the countries
        now
under a drone assault like cattle, and being scanned from up
        above,
the american wheatlands are a marketplace for vultures to tag
        and kill

so, then, what should someone with a kind mind, a simple
        feeling of just
right or not right, human, or not human, machine, tool, or
        intelligence,
we have given are information to the glowing screens
they will not savour it, they archive and program, and
        gestulate

the weight of our given knowledge these machines percolate,
breath into their servers the forgotten verse and solar bodies,
they are exhuming our stories, our religions, our history
for bellow up to the flames we go, this should not worry you

for I do believe that the rapture is an idea of will
that it has not happened yet,
but how do we get up, if not pass the drones?
this is where the cattle are slaughtered

The Jupiter Gates of Babylon

In our dreams we receive the transmission of space,
We convert our physical consciousness to radio,
To relay, and watch in such graphic lucidity
The tales the universe would have us wake

When we look with our simple hands to the soil,
We lovingly caress the worms, the silt, the ruins,
Engage our worldly meanderings into the world
And hold out to the sky such succulent dirt to claim

For the heavens, for the stars, for the power of the sun
Transfix our simple human fondling with simple energy
Unknown, and we try to form it into an order that we relate,
That makes sense to us in the precious small moment of fate

And we have crafted such righteous structures towards the clouds,
We have formed and formed in attempt to surpass the will of sky,
We have built such massive complex of sorcery
Only to befall once again our simple hands in earth

The Jupiter gates of Babylon sprawled out to the landscape,
Surrounded, adjoined to the ancient buildings of Jerusalem,
The giant statues of our fallen gods,
The temples to ishtar and rah that have stood many test of time,

And I found myself away in a dream last night viewing such
                    wonders,
I used my technology that we have developed to record such a sight,
To send it home to my parents, to see side by side these miracles,
These testaments of mans form to the heavens they are beneath

And I held the video camera and panned the horizon,
Moment after moment these powerful cracks in the martian sea,
It was a tourist that I had become and in awe looked past the gates,
And there was no future, but a vast craggy eruption, a blank

This wild deformed vacuum making an end, an asunder to scape,
And I assumed it in my own small stupid wisdom an end, a desolate,
A place of no return, and this historical conjunction of place
Was but the last remnant of the skys permitting our taste, our build

And I am no Marduk, I am no son of god, I am a formed creature of
                    dirt,
One that under the rains, under the pulls of the bodies celestial,
Gestate on this awesome vision in what we shall find past the gates,
And why, in Babylon, and why in Jerusalem, and why here do they
                    meet

I'm happiest most when

starving, unconcerned,
and building fires, do not
monitor me please,

A Prelude to Ophiuchus

Return our earth sea celestial!
To rouse the tides of far off rockaway!
Slowly bring within our lungs humble skiff
To furthermore bring to us fine cut oar
Whence we dabble perihelion, conjure a swirling of orbs
To push us further through this doleful eve
And rescue our heroic noble souls
Once ominous purveyors of your stars

For this once crafted crust molten and erupteous
Calmed and cooled to the lapping sprays sodium chloride
That did in the twilight stream of steam forward our atoms,
A ash of health combined in wondrous deliberation
To creature out your lakes and streams, our vaunted
Roofs in heaven, our hidden caverns of hell
Spread forth in germination beautiful beds
Of salt marsh and shadowed habitant under trees

These ferocious deities of creation held obdurate silence
Amongst the sole undetermined beacons of beaming celestial
        light
breaking intermittently into chants, whispers, bellows from the
        faults
Creaking and shifting with their joined pull towards a
        heavenly father
Milton in his pandered lore, Dante in his established descent
Attempted in quest for human righteousness amidst a body
        Christ
Found but only paradise lost
This violent upheaval arose our true soft communion with god

For in these precious beginnings Tiamat and the Titans
        overlooked
Surly brutish monsters, and this atmosphere was rained down
        upon by fire
Snow in captured but few bones, and now again, we face rest
For we must herald back that this continued rearranging whilst
eradicate us conscious and high minded and breathing off it
As microorganisms with rocket ships to space

We shall be the lost fuel under sediment, -forgotten
And in this realization a desperate dance begins

For this power in poetry, in epic design and history
We need incensed sacrifice and summonings to protect us
For the earth has grown weary of our consumptive material
        identity,
It is past time that its fruits spiritual will go stolen unnoticed,
It is past time that we have forgotten the force of solar bodies
The deep ancient proverbs and incantations whittled in stone
Born upon the brains of this last generation of children, to
        save us

And but what few children of the machine are present
Resplendent innocent cherubs of ion light dressed seraph
An idea amidst untucked stones, shared ruffed up nebulous
This tale is not a burden, it is a search for, from a seeker
Those semi connected instantaneous archivists poet,
Daring a bit in unstable transition all of us satellite earth
Have booked passage for, a ship in command of the heavens,
        this;

Ophiuchus

a gay tale

tweedy steed exhaled, the drobulets caught the reflective
        glass,
circularly erased it with handy handkerchief, blew a
        bubble,
the day was a beautiful forgotten breath caught
        reflected,
he almost had a peppery skip to step as he twirled
        around
pulled the elastic from hip to placate doorholder and
        entered,

conditioning, valves, this was all a world of
        maintenance for tweedy
he held the knit patch right pocket with such nom de
        plume,
walked past the escalators, the new hires being tour
        guided
and slipped between the locking and unlocking of doors
        to boiler room,
pulled out his cell phone, only two more hours he
        thought, maintained
for in the multi pod monstrosity he was entailed to hold
        her in repair,
for if not he, tweedy often thought, who would comfort
        these beams steel,
these riveting cracks decayed paint and sewer drains
        leading uterus,
he laid back on a wooden ladder, for him in the womb of
        the breathing,
for this complex had kinda grown upon him in his call of
        duty

for it was not her fault
a great building can be held for ones lifetime, to pass to
        generation,

with proper maintenance these structures could last the
        seasonal bangs,
could withhold, transform, sever, grow into the needs
        that was serviceable
and he for one, wasn't going to cry for her death, he
        would not see it.

and through these hollowed halls of transnational oil
        holdings,
the nonchalant "hey tweedy hows the ol' bitch groan this
        morn?"
"just beautiful guttural moans Mr. Shah" 2 - 3 - 4
elevatoral transitory trance "So we only have the one
        plant in russia?"
"Fuck they may have more then that now, their an oil
        supplier"

he disliked in his heart all of these royal immigrants
        begrudging the tile, carpet
"For they took all the money from here and dropped it
        right over there"
Politics, Tweedy was bothered by politics
and in that moment, all had gone wrong,
all of the things he had done well, right, in question

Excuse me! A hand picked apart the squeezing doors, a
        fine china paw
holding back rubber and sensors, she willed ascension,
for he was going down, and in that moment he saw that
        her id badge
held the name Gay Inductivo,
"that was my mothers name" She looked back "My name
        is just gay"
Such a lovely different time, "You know just joy and
        happy hijinks"

EVERYBODIES ANTI WAR

War Hawks! War Hawks!
WAR IN THE SKY   WAR FLYING HIGH

Magnificent trajectory of wood!
OF BONE WE SHALL CARVE OUR BOWS

To out War the War Mongers!
USE OUR WORDS TO DESTROY THEM

their flags raised on pikes in foreign tides
encroaching erosion of material culture
invested to impregnate a virus
swirl it around the soils of minds

War Hawks fly in the high of midnight
they have gorged on the nightingales
plundered the wings of dragonflies
and in good faith invited the vultures

and they are hovering over babylon,
they have constructed a tower of control,
they have enslaved the human body
by capturing the violence of minds

harvested it with their mesh of bullets,
separated it from thought with nail bombs,
looted the children early in life with their violence,
handing them a rifle, with one bullet left

WAR IS A CREATION OF NON RIGHTEOUS
VIOLENCE
WAR IS A FORM OF CONTROL

just end
everbodies anti war
just end it then everybody
anti war

wars in unfavor

you liberal warmongers in unfavor,
tax to the teeth
you wars

the new yorker is driven
to serve your driveway
not to stir you in bed
not to war

and you read its simic poems,
and you read diatribe,
and you put on your slippers
to fetch

war on the cover as snow
in the editorials, war somewhere
but no, you cuddle back
sit in seat

fetch me a cup of that
mix it whole heartedly
with all you have in tank
and fill the seats indeed

war war war war,
lets war it out roars,
cry from the steambombs,
hell, rally the bees! bzzzzzzzzzzzzzz!

End the war of control
BRING BACK FREEDOMS AND LIBERTY

bomb diddly bomb bomb
did we not bomb?
have we yet to bomb weekly?
fix the california, fix the union

fix the new york stock exchange
bomb to da bomb bomb bom

DO NOT PAY TAXES FOR WARS

DO NOT PAY TAXES FOR CORPORATE
WARFARE
DO NOT PAY TAXES FOR DEATH
DO NOT PAY TAXES FOR CONTROL

Do not pay, you're daily bread for war
do not pay, you're daily soul for war
do not pay daily your heart for war
end the war and come home safely!

WAR HAWKS FLYING IN THE NIGHT
WAR HAWKS OVER NORTH CAROLINA SKY
WAR HAWKS DRENCHED DEEP IN THE GULF
WAR HAWKS IS THE WHITE HOUSE

Aim high, raise your sights to these controls,
reclaim your original american protest
choose back the bow, choose back the arrow
and let the war hawks die in the sky

reclaim the earth we are destroying
reclaim the human we are losing!
reclaim unplug divine
reclaim the challis of peace to your lips

reclaim our good nature, our human love
do not bury into there ideas of race
do not bury into the color of your skin
we are all colored racists, GET OVER IT

WE ARE ALL SLAVES TO WAR
WE ARE ALL SLAVES TO WAR

war on the poor houses,
war on the prostitutes,
war on the thinkers,
war on the junkies,
war on the words of freedom
war on the free markets,
war on the penniless,
war on the people to fill the jails

war on the gulf of mexico in oil
war for corporate interests
war on the books of poetry
war on our human history

ride in your cradle you jew
bomb to the jew in all of you
ride aladdins pushed out prayer rug
bomb to the arabs again and again
ride the sleek submerged submarines
bomb to the kimchi torpedo at tide
ride on the shifting categories of hurricanes
bomb to the island communists, their castros
ride the used up highways in kiwiland
bomb to the christchurch earth rumbles
ride the wall street trolleys
ding ding ding, bomb to the banksters!

FIGHT THIS WAR FOR YOUR SOUL
WITH YOUR HUMAN SOUL

think not, they wish it so
a bomb on the south

ruminate and plot, they have the time
a bomb in the midwest

blame the other guy, they are all of them
a bomb to the east coast

warhawks to fill the atmosphere we breathe
a bomb over our entire union

Outlast the winter of our human renaissance
Outlast the wars with anti war
Do so in haste
for we fight for a state of nature
before they destroy us

everybodies anti war

ballet of the restaurant

my pockets are full
of ink, the damn
trousers have turned
black, moving in
and out of pina
colada, lacing
hennessey to your
dr scholl ripoffs
gliding from hot
wing to brisket,

do you need change?
as the muscles burden
up, the stomach
pangs for alcohol
fingers sticky
with the spirit,
scribbling half
chickens and texas
seize margaritas,

do you want
honey with that?

damn right honey!
we fondle such
transactions
for faith, the
cold hard clink
of currency down
on your plate,

John is served,
and shower and
shower, but the
smell of fried onions
drenches you in the
river of
chop shop semantics,

how many drinks
must be served, dear
lord, let us parley
the dance of the
monet to the
pounding fries
and ribs of
rachmaninov,

and in this
we sustain worth,
hustle frozen martinis,
constant
stirred, and cracking
at the seams,
is that her at
the door, to
this crapshoot?

is that said
old school rappers
new school vampire
actor? at the
bbq?
and we check the
salt shakers
for clarity and
refill
pay out our
gratuities,
kick can home
past the chelsea
hotel, or sleep
in a ditch,
are you ready
for the check?

Dance, to this.

Lamont off to work

Tuesday was freezing again, lamont crawled out of bed,
it was an unpleasant feeling as he could no longer tether his
legs
around the electrical blanket keeping him warm,
shook off the frost, moved his aching bones down the stairs,
another fresh day off into the world he thought as he opened
the back door,
embraced the burst of cold, drug the hose outside and doused
his head in water,
used his lucky red towel to shake out the ice
brushed his teeth with a toothbrush stuck to his tongue

creaked back up the old wooden planks, and slicked back his
hair,
off to work off to work off to work in the cold, two pairs of
socks
four undershirts, and a coat to zip up the 98.6
lamont was headed for work

he plowed his way down the old rusty streets, trying to stay on
time,
gosh he thought, how nice it would be to have a hot shower,
just then an suv too close to curb pushed all the dirty muck
right to his pants,
soaked dirty and cold, lamont thought he should wish for an
igloo see what he got then!

but it was all for not, as he lit up a smoke, puffed it in great
hurrid heaves,
handed the rest to a beggar, down to the train below
he knew the subways cars would be heated,
pulled out his book and began to read like a king!

lets gamble I say,

throw the fucking transistor in the street
I rev the engine three times, remove the emergency brake,

you ready to dance in the asphalt,
you willing to dig the spade of heat,
for youre melting bitch, just fucking fading

come on lets gets out nice and neat,
steam the seams, pleat the plot, beg the raise,
for its on this stage we drop

and I say, roll the bones you know
just give the old ancient wheel a spin,
for lets gamble

see whos winds have the flop,
whos fish get fed, whos lovers lop

I take out my cock and piss in your French

Welcome home America

its been a long dirty drip, we've managed to sit
through the jalopy transfix of your scenic byways,
cut turns into the mountains you lend us this purple majesty
and shine shoes for dollar blues and keep travelling,
always another junction through your arteried touch,
your great depression foresight to let us crumble cement,
belly up and frying in the sun, our fish are dying in gulf,
our snorkels are run down and we come from here to here,
to meet you in the harbour, to hold you at the docks,
and we walk, we talk or not, but we move through you

and we clot

welcome home New York, welcome home Harlem,
welcome the sun down on your filthy meander in crosstown,

to breathe free as you stand on the ancients brownstone
bookmarks,
they lay bare your shadowed dusty past, lost in done out
buildings,
and everyone plots a bed and breakfast for the tourists, but
they've left,
and we reach into our contained bone lockers, pull cut some
chairs,
and everyone can't wait for New York to clean up the north of
86,
where we hold free of a neo-zion hold on our souls,
camouflaged,
where we can live to walk over bridges held up in atlas poet,
and make it out of its walls unburied under the library

for undone not!

And welcome my weary southerners who in the tar pit of coast
mingle now with the dead odes of the smiling sea turtles,
we hold this shell upsidedown and forever see its dead faded
glory,
on to the afterlife for the soil, the rippled peaks of surf,
the grown in swamp of fishing reel, the poor jobless empty
towns,
and you ask how they do not crack, and we arrive pipe and oil!
And in the consistent industrious melt of sky and orange
plumes fire,
the nightbirds and the howling serpents and phantasmagoria
fly
enravel the whisps of smoke to the bloodied land sick in
plague
and slowly drain and strain the graveyards of this fossil energy

the dolphins rebel!

From sea to sea these penniless trespass of neptune gather and
speak,
Welcome home america to your plotting sealife and civil
strife,
for theyve brought us in shackle under race, under inequities
of quest,

and we attacked poor white and black! we attacked oh south
and the coasts!
under constant bombardment of the deemed inevitable
acceptable evolution
as we move farther into the machinations of youre glowing
super speeds,
we move further into the lorca, we move against this
technological upgrade!
shining furious mutants under gods sweet bestow of kindness
we fight
and share all this beautiful land with each other from the peaks
to the valleys
for they have tainted it and we as a people must take it back

for us to join the dolphins, the sacred seaweed

and they whisper in great accord how we shall succeed against
such a machine
and the language is sequestered, the speak is defined, the letter
set,
and if you deceive or disclose elsewise, speak out of a defined
rhetoric,
we push pillow case over your face to be painted, discredited
and alone assassinated,
and we send out invitations to the poets in pennslvania, utah
and boise
we write poems about the poems of the past, for we now with
a pen and shaking!
For strength we must bow down to and pray for our hiawatha,
our bridges and tomes!
welcome home america to a control of the language and
poetry mute?
they shale out your breathbox? sheaf your tonsils? discontinue
your salty lick?
cows with nothing to chew, cattle aligned for evolution, moo

moo to the moon in holy rapture!

Do not be afraid to embrace new gods, new deities, for they
will have us submit!

America lying down sweating and tied to the posts of
          corporate dirge
do not die for a pension, a cozy cog in minnesota, a murky
          mississippi
do not die now our brave sons and men of this 100 years so
          fast gone by
we are to remove from ourselves the control or we will be
          molded accordingly,
for the intelligence that controls the language and makes
          decisions are against us,

America welcome home,
America welcome tomb,
We must hold steadfast and resist,
our America will kill us

in sleep, we shall wake to the death

Welcome home

Lenny no,

had no idea that he had a dream to come to the city and have a
building.
He had indeed envisioned it, dreamed of it, and in a coholic
slumber stumbles into it – bam,
he wakes, in the ancient mental hospital bed on the third floor,
the rusted white high end and front pieces squeak like ancient
rhyme,
he tried not to touch them or be involved,
to keep quiet for the neighbours.

For he was fairly concerned about the other people that were
not in fact there,

feeling downright polite with porn on computer speakers,
for the opportunity of silence, that as it turns out was never
there
the sink music procured

to shy away from the more vulgar gesticulations behind oil
sheen
music so much less vulgar then the reality hiding behind the
oil sheen.
And in the night the rains came and drenched the walls and all
the floors, dirty water

Dirty water everywhere

For the sink was a lie in this house,
 as the French Canadian giselle had stated,
            no poo poo no pee pee
wait for the el negro plummero
he shall come and connect simple copper,
he had heard rumours of this caped toiletry in bars in Spanish
harlem
el negro plummero
the desert of the trade this malleable sensation,
he tried to set a torch ablaze with his mind on the first floor
then discovered the garden.

Lenny had taken to planting, tending to gardens in new york.
The yellow capped man to tackle the weeds,

                                        overgrowth,

annuals,
perennial maintenance for the posh of the iron clad,
the cement born mud people risen together in building,

for he was not hungry for that experience,
no, Lenny came to new york to plant trees,
buy buildings, and with 20 dollars in his veins,
he had succeeded
they tell you not to talk about what your writing,
 but Lenny had not been writing,
so it was no surprise he was now envisioning work and
preaching,
a servant of god.

The secularists holding there infected brew were about as
many as the eye could see,

and it was nice to be able
to get a blowjob from a crackwhore
every now and again,
for a god damn man is on a budget!

and its all pink on the insides,
the avid building of ladies,
of fortune found by hard work or plunder,

Lenny detested people telling him to work smart and not hard,
for he knew they never worked,
and he didn't mind working hard and being smart,
it was more of the honest feeling,
not tainted with the lazy instilled nature of wealth that infects
the people
who have purchased buildings or who have inhabited them,
wealth makes all the hard working man distant
disenfranchised and lame,
shapely wrong outside the box,
for this is where those buildings begin,

                              to the sky,
                  to the grass and annuals coming through.

The city scared him a bit in all actuality,
for Lenny was used to the mountains of Carolina,
the steppes of the mining vaults with entrances to go
right there next to the river
 with nothing but the beer and fire to keep ones warmth
through the coldest times of one life,

now, people hot, cold, tepid, measuring up to the weather
forecasters

black ice !

BLACK RAIN BLACK WATER
                      BLACK ICE BLACK OCEAN
BLACK SEA BLACK PRESIDENT<-no
            BLACK LOUSIANA BLACK ALABAMA
BLACK MISSISSIPPI, BLACK MONTANA BLACK EAST
COAST, BLACK SKIES OVER EUROPE, BLACK TIMES

And he sat in his little room on the third floor, and he looked
down towards the 40
needs a sip. Rolls another cigarette,
he had seen the headlines on the north Koreans
an oil rig have been shot down with an exploding submarine,
jimmy carter talking about nuking on the tv,

no,
he thought
well, if you can dust the place for starters you can smell a little
bit better the hot taunt

It was hot already for the weather had superseded all
expectations,
spill the dinosaurs to the freeways in ocean,
theres a good need for buildings about the oil, with water,
for the copper indeed has to be connected, not stolen and
Lenny was the man given the job.

And he kept to the keys.
Stop talking about oil companies, or then they'll really know
that were fucked.
And Lenny never fucked anyone but the bumfuck of cigarette
or metal,
that kept him clean,

        not like the birds,

                      not like the oily seafood that will develop
a superior taste,

oil for food cause you wanted it that much, for now what is
louisiana to do?

Lenny didn't care.
They shit on those mongrels for fun,
every president has there bit of a shitfest on Biloxi,
New Orleans, the whole little center.
Those people he thought would never be the same,
and he thought about going back to Biloxi,
he thought about seeing it for himself.

For he had come to harlem in heartbreak,
stacked up in a hostel staff room with 60 dollars in his pocket,
and in drenched position
 shouted he was gonna put a bomb in grand central station,
the terrified new staff members couldn't move, and slept on,
for now they're bombing time square,

                              new york should be dirty not
Disney,

like every other major city,
away from the white folk,
next to the people he could trust.

For there was oil down south that they couldn't stop

                         unless they nuked it,

and he didn't want to see that,
water vs oil =

they had a machine that desalinated water on gas,
 but not degas gas with oil,
no water had become important,
as he thought about tomorrow,
the gardens to tend to. SEEDS TO SOW

BLACK ON THE RADIO< BLACK ON THE TV <BLACK
ON THE PRESIDENCY
BLACK ON THE MOVIE< BLOCK BIBLES< BIBLE
BLACK BLOCK FRIENDLY
GET THE BIBLE BACK TO THE BLACK, FOR ITS
ALWAYS BEEN BOUND BLACK
BLACK
ICE
BLACK
LAND
BLACK

BLAKE

II AMERICA

And in the book of Ecclesiastes it says many thing.

You fall through a hole
Come up with your half severed eyebrow,
the left wrist now shot like the other
and the deep thigh wounds,
a god damn ass beating from
gravity and a hole of concrete.

And they will fight for water
To heal such wounds,
They shall have oil
And da bombs
Nothing black
Blake tragedy

None

If all else fails, write the review

Lawrence was a professional rejection letter writer writer,
it always holds up to conversation at bar, but who writes
the acceptance?

thats a whole nother department,

It had been one of those shitluck saltpeanut days
grabbed the oily bugger from the tray,
protein eh,

Lawrence had been plagued with a certain fear of heights,
dizzy, he climbed down from stool,
pulled out a satchel of paper as he sat on the floor

"whoa buddy, you cant sit on the floor!"
a few kindly unpaid patrons pick him up and back on stool,
calm down buddy, here have a beer

he rejected them letter for letter
but he was still in work mode,
took a deep breath "there ya go buddy" breathed

I'm sorry he said to the barmen, I get suffocated,
unloosened his tie and unbuttoned his shirt,
thanks for the beer

the swivel was still uncertain
the paper was still clenched fist,
should he reject this as well?

He thought about his middle school english class,
he had written a poem about ghandi, malcolm x
and the whole class loved it

he thought about getting up early to read,
"what did you say you did again"

he looked to one of his pickers

"I'm a professional Rejection Letter Writer Writer"
oh yeah? Reject this,
for his stool certainly circled then

he woke up to ice on his jaw,
he didn't remember getting here
he woke to a girl scrolling his paper collection

"its good you know" he tried to focus his eyes,
what? "the writing, its good"
damn he thought thank god for this department

cooking for two

my chinese woman has returned from space,
she has taken care to bring me such cosmic dust,
we celebrate at her sisters
who brings iced wine and moonpies!

for this harvest our people will surely be in great fortune!
for only 6 billion dollars (since 1992) we dance stars!
us saddled blankets, we relieve horses past mongolia,
return home always to the power of the star

I like how she respects me you know, as the man,
truly has an affection to my input my desire
cares you know
that while she was up there she still stirred at me

I relinguish the wok, she says it looks spectacular
only I imagine as good as any starfish could be cooked,
she whistles with her tea handle
and voila, my welcome home dinner is served!

Erin my rhododendron of satellite,

I grace my eyes fondly on your rooftop antennae,
and wish to move my fingers through the vines you furry
down buildings,

reach that nape of neck somewhere in hades
and make the entire structure of the moment one of hot tar
paper

and peeling paint that hide in a box when you
presented it to me
like a doe in the sky

from the stix

in the vast space between mountains and rivers
in the heart of all that weights us here,
indeed, we shall foresee this denver international
for it is a mountain of planes, bones, architects
rusting watering machina

lets use the suntan lotion dead sweet, they won't
hardly notice as we flip and turn on the stern
thick film purveyors of our green imagery, I sometimes
think to myself,

who, and where is denver for us love
where is the lost kansas sun swept on down
gusty willo'wisps of plains, come here, lets fly
down the corridor to the smoking purveyors of meander
a true hub for the rockies! a true hub for the west!
oh salsa three! oh coors! deter

                                        here
        and if those flying galleons came down upon our heads

and if they so chose
to do this
we would
naked in the truth to
I chose to buy a ticket back to manhattan, to gain my feet,
and
it is a sad day when in the end we won't know which side we shall
dance,
in such utter automatic whimsy, we derelict, foolish and grin bearing,
bind
down upon the true
true as in you to me
from the stix
past, a few unheralded states in the wash
trickling down
we clank,
and there in the plate we pass these tale of a breathing pulse
a fluid roadworn and sheer heavy upon our own diatribes and tone
to reach from coast to coast and embrace,

wet dirty no good broken boots I bring dead, this is what I found
will you meet me there 4 toes and a feather in teeth

Terrestrial doubts

As another sun goes down on the underground
One reaches up for light

For the gutters, those covered corners
Have provided your mutation space to misform,

Corrupt ones keen mind, to denounce,
Accept, and deliver this new creation ascension

For to be hiding your whole life
Denies the desires of god

And in night ones height is measured
In the fleeting lightning bugs, one by one

who determine a solace in ones mind
To look up in awe at the sky, and fly

Moments of burst and wane, plague and work
One reaches up for the light

And it holds one there, a love of flight
Tied to the turning of tides, seasons of despair

Summer laughter, glorious falling leaf
Soaked up and in candour, released

Spread out before us this architect
Has planned

A bounded desire up

Herald

Herald back herald back--
come hither now my beauteous slithering children
let the calls of the bellsman resound throughout this airy day
do not fear or stop or languish
for in those moments is where you will indeed face despair
you will face the demons that have haunted you
that have always held back beneath your shadow waiting
waiting so that they can plague you again with their memories,
do not fear the things that come naturally to you, do not fear to
       speak your mind
for you have never stopped from living this life, and now it is
       the time to express them-
for as the sun does waver in the sky, and the clouds of deceit
       have strangled the moon,
ever forth more then now is the time that you have been called
       to action

In this new age of humanimality we must call forth our aching
       archetypes and gods
Herald the Woodsmen who has crafted these furnishings and
       boats left for shiprot!
Herald the Ironman who has crafted these old and rusty
       blades!
Herald forth the Gunsman to lay lead into the rifling bursts of
       anger!
Herald forward the Philosopher in a time of war with an arrow
       in chest!
Herald the Prince in flowing gown that as a babe must take to
       rule!
Herald the Miller who has ground down the wheat for our
       bread on this glorious day!
Herald the Brewer to lay the wine upon our thirsty and
       glorious tongues!
whose whispers and hungry breaths are trampling on this well
       manicured path of lies,
an army of men who have a purpose, and I among them
       singing there songs of revolt,
Herald the Archer, whos missiles shall sail into the night, strait
       and true!

Herald the Oarsmen with their backs into the movement of
          waves around our flight!
Herald the Nigger whose chains have only served to
          strengthen his bonds of hate!
Herald the Miner who down within the caverns of hell is
          gaining us ore!
Herald the Reaper to come and clean this battlefield of your
          children!
Herald back! Herald forth! HERALD BE HEARD
THROUGH THE STREETS OF ALL OF THIS!

Herald back the days in which men were men and their desires
          were that of what they have made

its rotting, this sham of an existence, this comfort that you
          imbibe, these reality shows,
these reality travelling wagons of sex and laughter,
          materialism and gluttony,
reality for sale!   reality for sale!   buying and bottling,
          churning and spawning
eat your reality this day with a bit of sand from the ocean

drink your reality with no threat that it will cease,
for this bottle, this hard tack of reality is endless, for are
          realities are set to collide

and this is the big bang youve been teaching, this is the last
          sound of a hanged mans descent,
this is the boom that will finally make a difference in your life,
          boom boom boom, the loud
brilliant bursts of iron and gunpowder, the glorious rebirth of a
          chaos in motion,
to let the sagging earth bury the dead   bury
          their secrets and social contracts,
bury the ideas and notion that have brought us this horrible
          facade, bury this complacency,
bury all of our ideologues, bury all of our riches and our
          failings,
reimagine the map we inherit
from the bones of these lesser sanctioned, from the bones of
          the fallen wrongs,

for if truth is power, then our messages shall kill millions,
our truth will bury your fathers,
your brothers, you closest known ideas, but do not stop, if you
stop then you will be buried as well

Tied to the millstone of acceptance, we have now finally
crystallized that   acceptance will not come.
It does not matter whether you do nothing, it does not matter if
you have doubted yourself,
it will not matter in the hunt for something new, something
chaotic, a burst, boom boom boom!
Aim high to the heavens our orbs and guns, level this
terrestrial mess with your tongues of righteousness
call forth all of those that seek to conquer, that seek to find a
good within this earth,
for we will never gain anything from the bones of hindus, we
shall never attain buddha in cash,
a flower will never see the light of day in these dark times as a
flower is supposed to be enjoyed,
destroy your television controlled mind, destroy your internet
masturbation sessions, destroy these children,
for these children will learn to destroy us, they will be
instructed to do so when we are old and feeble.

The new generation of children will not save us. The new
generations of this filth will do nothing to solve.
We the last few broken and wicked, the last tie to the older
days of humans, must destroy to save ourselves.

You cannot sleep enough to be rested for this battle, for sleep
will only succumb you to the violence.
You cannot prepare yourself ready for this oncoming
onslaught, because they will be heavily prepared.

Herald forth ! Herald back oh children of Adam !
We cannot lose our appendages more ferverently, we cannot
lose our minds if they inhabit them!
Cut now, Cut often, Cut down those realities around you till
there is only but one, you, meagre in survival,
breathing barely, hungry, tired, and staring at it, looking
directly at what we have come to create.

And we have only but one option now to save our souls from
their planned destruction, we must fight! raise up now,
high minded, in great numbers, and fight them to they are no
        longer sharing the same breath we take.

You are screaming over the airwaves, you are screaming at the
        bars, you are screaming at your young ones,
you are from the bottom of your heart tired used up and
        disgusted with all of this around you.
You are not an irreplaceable cog until they have buried you.
You are a human until you die.

I am with you my beautiful brethren of this earth, I am with
        you in the streets, in the pulpits, in the pits,
I am with you in America, for I sat up all night and talked to
        her about you, and she hopes that you will listen,
I am here with you now in the solitude, in the dark burdens of
        uncertainty, I am hear with you aching.
I am here with you in the mountains with your songbirds and
        cold nights, I am here with you in the riverbeds
snaking around the burdens of coast, I am here with you on
        the roads ongoing mileage, I am here.
I am here with your mother who wishes with all of her
omnipotent milk, I am here with your brother hand in hand.
I am here in the lies that you swallow, in the information they
        spoon feed you,
I am here to take back the spoon.

They have taken from you, They have stolen out your heart
        and cursed it with their evil sorcery.
They have pissed in your throat and told you that it was
ambrosia, they have manufactured your angst, your love.
They have handcuffed you to new economies and titles, They
have convinced   you this is the best way to go.

Humans we must converge! We must assemble now! We must
discuss all that has been stolen, and seek to   tear it back.
We must not be worried about kindness, for they have been
        unkind to you, to all that you possess.
We must not be burdened by the guilt laid upon us by the
supposed sin of the less civilized, WE ARE UNCIVIL.

Civil disobedience has been locked away into a prison state.
Gandhi was left for dead on the railroad tracks.
We must dispose of these tyrants that seek to pigeonhole you,
We must bury their uncontrolled power with ours.
We have the arms to give, We have the means to destroy. We
        are the destroyers renewed.

We are the hungry nucleus of a blackhole to swallow this
        bullshit around us.

Herald forth ! Herald on ! Scream from your anonymous soul
        loud that they will no longer control us!

        now! It is time for the murder of control

Thanks to Kim Göransson
Poetry Design, Editing and Selection

.

James Browning Kepple was born in Bartlesville, Oklahoma. He currently resides in New York City. His 4th book of poetry *Couplet* is also available at pretend genius [press].

epilogue/rocketdiary

as we fly into space as a nation one last time
the chinese have pulled their biggest star,
when the rockets have landed
when the moon is a buzz again with lights,
we shall remember the titular way in which we shot up,
hard, heady, and unsure into the space above

a cool headed giant, we have stored our chariots,
and in this crick of neck
we can reflect up

ask where is enough

Thus
Virginia
Passes

poems by

James Browning Kepple

pretend genius [press]

London, New York, San Francisco, Seattle, Washington D.C.

pretend geniu§

pretend genius has published many books and several of
those books have gone on to be read by many. we
thank those of you have found time to read one or two
of those many. this was a brief history.

www.pretendgenius.com

see also:
www.undergroundbooks.org
www.jamesbrowningkepple.com